My All For Him

Other books by the same author:

Behold His Love
Father of Comfort
Hidden in His Hands
I Found the Key to the Heart of God,
    autobiography
Mirror of Conscience, booklet
My All for Him
Praying Our Way Through Life, booklet
Realities of Faith
Ruled by the Spirit
Those Who Love Him
You Will Never Be the Same

Susan Burt

My All For

Him

Basilea Schlink

BETHANY HOUSE PUBLISHERS
MINNEAPOLIS, MINNESOTA 55438
A Division of Bethany Fellowship, Inc.

Published by
BETHANY FELLOWSHIP, INC.
6820 Auto Club Road
Minneapolis, Minnesota 55438

English edition originally published 1971
by Marshall, Morgan & Scott, London

First German edition 1969

Original title: Alles für Einen

ISBN 0 87123 370 3
PRINTED IN THE UNITED STATES
OF AMERICA

Foreword

This is a book for our times. This is a period in which, because of wars, clashing ideologies, scientific advance and swift social changes, the West has floundered in its relationships both as regards people and the world. Psychiatry may tell us that love is the unifying factor, but it cannot supply the ability to love. Sadly enough, the Church, which should supply a love-hungry world with what it hungers for, does not convince the world that it has Christ's love.

In this book Mother Basilea takes us into the heart of loving, which is to love Jesus and to be loved by Him who is the source of all love. She describes how love for Jesus reached a point in her where it set her free from both people and the world. Then, being free, she was able to love and appreciate both.

As I read this book, my heart yearned to love our Lord more. But it yearned most hopefully! For Mother Basilea does not merely express the depth of her own love for Jesus. She also shows how we too may ourselves experience it deeply.

There is no easy religion here, praise God. The insistence from the outset is that Jesus must be our *first* love. He must come before everyone and everything else. Here is described first-hand, vital, all demanding discipleship, but not as an ideal possible only to the few—for it depends not upon our abilities, but upon our Lord's love burning in our hearts.

The touch of the mystic is here, as it must be from the pen of someone who loves Jesus so much. She expresses revealingly what this love can mean to the soul, but lofty and real as her writing is, it is also clear and simple, so that we feel that we too can be led along this road by the Holy Spirit.

This book will warm the hearts of those who long to love

our dear Lord more. It will show them how to experience
the love of the Bridegroom in a way which, at present, may
be only a longing. In doing this, it will meet the greatest
need of today. As the forces of darkness move forward,
nothing but the sufficiency of the love of Christ filling our
hearts will be great enough to triumph against them. We
need to be shown the way while there is time.

R. W. East

The Vicarage,
West Mersea,
Colchester.

Contents

Should someone be unable to comprehend some of these truths or expressions, may he retain at least that which he can recognize as sound and seek to practise it. With time everything else will become clear and lucid for him. Those whom these things do not suit, may they leave them to those who love them, and may they be careful lest they blaspheme against things which they do not understand.

—Gerhard Tersteegen, 1697–1769

What these pages contain are not thoughts about the "first love", the bridal love, for Jesus, but rather what I myself have experienced along the path of love for Jesus. This is a reality. I can and must bear testimony about the truth of this verse: "Whom have I in heaven but thee? And there is nothing upon earth that I desire besides thee" (Psalm 73: 25). Lord. You are everything!

—Basilea Schlink

One Thing Is Needful

Probably never before was this one thing so needful as today: the "first love" for Jesus. Only when we have this love shall we be able to survive the difficult times which lie ahead of us. The world has never known such times as these. Already in this century more Christians have been martyred than in all the previous centuries. We are living in a time of great apostasy, in a time of temptation. Who can prevail when temptation comes or when martyrdom draws close? Only he who has the "first love" (Rev. 2: 4). This love characterized the first Christians. Many of them suffered martyrdom out of passionate love for Jesus; yes, it was their love which impelled them to embrace it, and to suffer for His sake.

We see, then, the power of this "first love". It is stronger than the power of suffering, which otherwise might depress us and render us hesitant, cowardly, incompetent and despondent. We need this first love in order to persevere. Only one power is stronger than the power of suffering, and that is this divine life of love. God is love. Wherever He pours out His divine life into human hearts, men begin to love Him intimately and fervently, and nothing, absolutely nothing in the world, not even the greatest sufferings or horrors, not martyrdom itself, can erase this divine life. This divine life is immortal.

First love—precious gift! First love—the one thing needful. First love—we should desire it, pray for it and seek to attain it at any cost. According to the Scriptures there is another name for this first love. It is called bridal love, because Jesus calls Himself the Bridegroom (Matt. 9: 15). The Scriptures also speak of the "marriage" and the "marriage supper" of the Lamb, to which we are invited, and of the bride of the Lamb, who has made herself ready (Rev. 19: 7–9). The bride is the whole host of the elect, and each member must possess this bridal love.

The words of scripture show that love between bridegroom and bride here on earth is but a shadow of the love between the heavenly Bridegroom and His bride. Compared with this first, strong, exclusive love for Jesus, every human love fades into nothingness. This first love is called bridal love, because it is undivided like the love of a young bride. She has given her heart to her bridegroom, and so here Jesus is the Bridegroom who receives an undivided love.

First love or bridal love is of prime importance today, for Jesus is going to return soon. When He comes, He will come as the King and Bridegroom to seek His bride and take her to Himself. He will come only for those souls who are on fire with bridal love for Him. These indeed are the only souls who are filled with an eager desire to prepare themselves for the Bridegroom and for the marriage of the Lamb.

This bridal love, which we need so much, is not an unattainably high goal; it is within our reach. It comes from Jesus Himself; it is an expression of His nature, of His innermost being. Because He first loved us, He has already planted the seed of this love within our hearts. Love is the greatest power on earth, and because this divine love is so fervent, so pure, so intimate, it has power to accomplish everything. It possesses the greatest authority, because it comes from the heart of Jesus. It is the power which constrained Him to suffer for the redemption of the world. This love impels us to sacrifice and makes us strong to endure suffering. It can impart such strength to us, because it unites us with the almighty Lord of heaven and earth.

One day, in the heavenly places, we shall discover—if we cannot realize this now—that this first love, bridal love, is the only thing worth desiring in our life of faith. Yes, it was for this love that we were created and redeemed. Only this can bring true joy into our hearts and reveal the meaning of true discipleship. Jesus is waiting for this first love, for this bridal love; He calls Himself the Bridegroom.

We love, because He first loved us.
1 John 4: 19

First Love — The Great Discovery

For a long time I could not find the key, the solution, to my questions: What is true discipleship? What does Jesus want? On the one hand, He calls us to an uncompromising discipleship. He calls us to forsake everything, to lose our lives for His sake. He calls us to leave father and mother. On the other hand, we are supposed to honour our fathers and mothers. In the same way, the Bible says that the whole creation is God's handiwork; thence springs human knowledge and science, and thus our civilization: surely we should hold it in esteem? Now, if we forsake all things to tread the path of uncompromising discipleship, we become ascetic and seclusive, denying civilization and everything that God has created. Yet this cannot be right! What are we to do?

Many voices reached my ears, and many sought to convince me that their way was right. One view was that as the body of Christ, we should not concern ourselves with what is happening in our country, or with human institutions of our times. We should take no account of the worlds of art, music and literature, not even of nature; we should live in one realm only—the Word of God and the fellowship of believers.

I listened to this but then I discovered that those who held this view lacked joy, that they did not give thanks to the Father for His benefits to us and did not appreciate the revelation of His greatness which nature affords. Furthermore, I often found these people narrow-minded, inhibited, stern and austere, and lacking love for others. At the same time, they were very self-righteous, because they thought that they alone had the truth.

Then I heard a very different view, and this too I explored. I found people who were more open-hearted and

14

more loving, more natural and relaxed. I discovered more of the radiance of Jesus in their lives and personalities than I had found in the others. These people did not insist that they alone were the body of Christ; actually they did not speak very much about their conversion and they took their place in the world. It seemed to me, however, that they had so fully conformed to the world that they did not pay attention to the warnings of scripture, e.g., "Do not love the world or the things in the world" (1 John 2: 15), "Do not be conformed to this world" (Rom. 12: 2), "Do not be mismated with unbelievers" (2 Cor. 6: 14). They seemed to ignore the scriptural injunction to take the way of Jesus, the way of the cross and renunciation.

Still I wondered. What did God want? Which was His way? I wanted to tread His path, no matter what it cost. After following first the one path for several years and then the other, I still did not feel that I had found His way. But He did answer my plea that I might find the right road and one day receive the glorious things that He had prepared. He had to make me see the truth about myself before He could show me the right way. He had to show me that I was a poor sinner. I had to become so desperate that I could cry over my sins. I could not get on with a difficult woman with whom I was living. I was frustrated, bitter; I could not see any way out. We seemed to be hopelessly at odds.

Then the Lord showed me my sin. He showed me that I was unloving and unmerciful towards my friend. He also showed me that I should have been able to win her over by overflowing compassion. Now I recognized that I was at fault. The Lord granted me a penitent and crying heart. This experience drove me into the arms of Jesus, for Jesus and the repentant sinner belong together. He began to reveal Himself as Love. It was He Himself—not any particular teaching or any religious doctrine, but rather He Himself who was the answer. My intellectual questions began to fade into the background. Only one thing was important: I was drawn to love Him who had forgiven me my sins, redeemed me and loved me so ardently. He became my greatest and my closest friend.

For me He had become the "fairest of the sons of men" (Psalm 45: 2). He was the jewel of my heart. He was the joy of all joys. He was the most precious object of my life. With Paul Gerhardt I could raise my voice in song:

> God is the Greatest, the Fairest, the Best.
> God is the Sweetest and the most Dependable.
> The most noble Treasure of all is He.

He truly is the sweetest—He of whom the psalmist writes: "Thou givest them drink from the river of thy delights" (Psalm 36: 8). I had drunk from this river, and it led me to love Him more and more.

My love for Him helped me to find the answer to my questions. I had found the key—love for Jesus, this first love, bridal love. Through this love I saw that to tread the path of Jesus does not involve abstention from the riches of our Father's world. All at once I noticed the two phrases which Jesus always added whenever He called someone to uncompromising discipleship: "For My sake", "For My name's sake". We are called to tread His path and be close to Him *out of love* for Him. One of the characteristics of true bridal love is the desire to be as close as possible to the beloved.

After the Lord showed me that the way of uncompromising discipleship is the way of voluntary love, He let me find the key to Christian freedom. Because Jesus is Love, He must have enjoyed hours of relaxation with His disciples. He drew their attention to the beauty of nature: "Consider the lilies of the field . . ." (Matt. 6: 28). They rejoiced over the Father's gifts. I began to comprehend this; now that I was joined with him in love, I could enjoy creation.

Now the gifts of the Creator were no longer strange and foreign to me, nor were they something to be avoided lest they draw me away from strict discipleship. Now they were a loving greeting from God the Father. I could enjoy them fully; they made me love Him more; they made me thank Him more. I could rejoice over all the beauty of art and civilization. I was no longer in danger of becoming bound to them; they would not now deter me from following the path of uncompromising discipleship. Rather, they led me into a deeper love for Jesus, they increased my gratitude to the Father, and they enhanced the effectiveness of my ministry.

Now everything had taken on a different appearance. Previously, when I was trying to lead an ascetic life, I scarcely dared to travel, but now I was free to travel. Now the motivation was different. In order to give God the glory, I undertook "praise trips" to scenic places erecting, in the midst of the beauty of creation, monuments inscribed with verses from Scripture. On such "praise trips" we would raise our voices in song to worship the God of creation. I was able thus to lead others to love and thank and praise Him. Previously, too, I scarcely dared to admire religious art. But, now when I saw pictures of Jesus or of the marvels that God had brought into being in lands where I had met Him, they aroused deeper thanksgiving and greater love in my heart, and helped me to glorify Him more in my ministry.

I no longer felt as though I had been separated from my fellow-citizens, that as an individual I might find salvation. No, now I loved my people and all other peoples, because they shared the radiance of the Father's love; they were a creative thought of His heart. Now, I could share God's suffering when our countrymen turned from Him and disregarded His commandments. According to the testimony of the Holy Scriptures, although the Father's heart was inclined towards His chosen people, it was also filled with grief over the doom which threatened the heathen city Nineveh (Jonah 4: 11). So I lamented now over our people because of their impending judgment.

Yes, all my questions had been answered and all my problems solved. Now I was truly free. I had feared that I might be caught up either in a way that was too narrow or in a way too conformed to that of the world. Neither seemed to be the true path of discipleship. Now I was really free as a child of God, because I was completely filled with His love. Now I belonged utterly to the One who is the heart of the universe and who contains everything in Himself. In the fellowship of love with Him I now had part in everything that belongs to this earth and to the whole universe. My love had become all-comprehending, but my love had also remained close to God and bound to the centre of creation.

The Faithful shall live with Him in love.
Wisdom of Solomon 3: 9 (AV)

Just as my life had been unhappy and torn with inner conflicts before I found this answer, so everything was much more happy and more natural afterwards. My life was filled with joy, because I had found the One who loved my soul and whom I was permitted to love above all else with all my soul, with all my strength, with all my being. I found in Jesus my greatest Love, my most intimate Friend, and for almost thirty-five years since then I have gone through life with Him, and over and over again I have told Him how much I love Him, who is my Bridegroom.

The Precious Secret of
Bridal Love for Jesus

There is a love which outshines all other loves—a love of unimaginable beauty, strength and fervency, which the singer of the Song of Solomon praises. "How fair and how pleasant art thou, O love, for delights!" (Song of Solomon 7: 6 AV). It is the love which Jesus bestows upon a bridal soul, and it is the love of the bridal soul for Jesus. It is unspeakable and wonderful that there is such a thing as this love, that Jesus loves us so much!

We can understand Him coming to us as a Redeemer, because we sinful men need a Redeemer, and it is natural for us to thank Him for this. We know too that He came to us as a physician to heal our infirmities of body and soul. He revealed Himself to us as the King of kings, the Lord of all hosts of cherubim and billions of angels, as a matchless Ruler clothed with majesty and divine power, at whose command demons fled and the powers of nature ceased their raging. For all these things people of all times have sounded their gratitude, their adoration, their praise and honour to Jesus, their Redeemer and Saviour, their Lord and King.

But, it is beyond our understanding that He wills not only to be King, Lord, Redeemer and Physician, but also the Bridegroom of sinful men. It is beyond our imagination that He as God wants to forge the bonds of love with sinful men, as He did with His chosen people, Israel, when He said: "I will betroth you to me for ever . . ." (Hos. 2: 19)—"Your Maker is your husband'" (Isa. 54: 5). Jesus wants to betroth Himself to the "bride of the Lamb". He wants to secure the bonds of love with her, with each individual soul that is a member of this host, whether it be man or woman.

This is a Great Mystery — I Take it to Mean Christ and the Church.

(from Eph. 5: 25–32)

Jesus, who so often says "Whoever loves Me . . ." "Do you love Me?" is concerned about our love.

He is concerned about a special kind of love. It is the love which is shadowed in the relationship between a bride on earth and her bridegroom; that is, it is an exclusive love, a love which places the beloved, the bridegroom, above all other loves, in the first place. As a Bridegroom, Jesus has a claim to such "first love". He who has loved us so much wants to possess us completely—with everything we are and have. Jesus gave Himself wholly and completely for us. Now His love is yearning for us to surrender ourselves and everything that we are and have completely to Him so that He can really be our "first love". If we offer Jesus anything less than this "first love", than the love which takes priority over all the other loves of our heart, He will not accept this. So long as our love for Him is a divided love, so long as our heart is bound to family, possessions, or the like, He will not count our love to be genuine. Divided love is of so little value to Him that He will not enter into a bond of love with such a soul, for this bond presupposes a full mutual love. Because our love is so precious to Jesus, because He yearns for our love, He waits for our uncompromising commitment.

Whenever there are two alternatives, true love always chooses Jesus. If, for example, Jesus calls someone into the mission-field, then for Jesus' sake he has to depart from his native land, often leaving his family behind or being separated from his wife for a while. The love for these things has to take second place. Jesus can be our true love, our first love, only if this love takes priority over all others, if, whenever we are faced with the choice between Jesus or people and things, we choose Him.

Jesus has the right to make such a claim upon our love, because there is no one like Him. No one is so full of glory, so full of royal beauty and powerful love as Jesus. His love is so overwhelming, so tender and so intimate, so fiery and strong. No human love could ever be compared with it. No one loves so exclusively, so faithfully and with such loving care. No one exists so exclusively for us as Jesus. Jesus knows what He can bestow with His love. He knows how happy He can make a human soul. That is why He has a thousand times more right than an earthly bridegroom to say, "Give Me everything—your whole love—your first love, for which you would leave earthly things behind, just as a bride would put aside all her other desires and would give up home and fatherland."

Jesus stands before us as One who entreats. He demands our love. He wants to take complete possession of us. His love is a jealous love, because it is so great and filled with such a strong ardour for us (Exod. 34: 14). It is a grief to Him when we do not return His love with all that we are and have. His love for us is so powerful that it yearns to receive the ultimate of love from us, and for the true bride there is nothing more blissful than to surrender her whole being, her whole love to the One who loves her. Indeed, if her Bridegroom takes her completely into His possession, it is bliss for her.

Divine possession—blessed words! God has taken possession of me. He longs for me so utterly that He is not satisfied until I give myself wholly and completely to Him. Only he who loves Jesus in this way can comprehend Jesus in His deepest nature, for only the soul that has given itself to Him completely in love can experience His great and intimate love.

We remember the rich young ruler. Jesus loved him, and the rich young ruler longed for the love-relationship to God. Jesus saw his deep desire to enter into this fellowship of life and love with God. (God is both life and love, and whoever gains eternal, that is, divine life, enters also into this love.) Jesus showed the young man the way to this greatest gift. Even people who are in many ways living a life of sin, and caught up in temporal things, desire a life of true fulfilment, that relationship of love to God which makes our lives blissful.

So Jesus showed him the way: to attain the precious pearl, eternal life, one has to sell something, one has to give up something—indeed, one must give up everything. This is inevitable, because the divine, eternal life is loving and this loving must be whole-hearted. In order to give my whole love to Him, I have to forsake other things I love.

The rich young ruler went away sorrowful, and to this day (as I have known for myself), we believers are often dismal and depressed. We have not been caught up into His great joy, because the heartfelt, blissful relationship of love to Jesus is lacking. So long as we cannot bring ourselves to give Jesus our first love, we shall not know this relationship. It may be that some are afraid of falling into false asceticism or legalism, but it is usually because we are chained to our earthly possessions, to our honour, to our profession, to people we love, and so on. We will not give Jesus our undivided love.

When I gave Jesus everything—not only a dedication in spirit, but when I truly put Him before people I loved, before my intellectual fancies and things that I prized—then the joyful life in the love-relationship to Jesus began. He revealed His love to me as a Bridegroom and gave me eternal life.

Jesus said to the rich young ruler: "Sell—give up—follow Me—bind yourself to Me and My way! Out of love give Me your life and everything that makes it rich and desirable for you. Give it to Me—not as an ascetic act, no, out of love! and I will give you the eternal, divine, overflowing life of love, which is the richest way of all, and which will make you abundantly happy. For only I can grant the highest life."

Jesus can say this, because He is "the Life". Whoever follows Him, whoever joins Him, is joined to that Life, to the stream of life and love that flows without end.

Yes, whoever follows Him receives eternal life. That is what I found. For years I had lived on "cheap grace"—not answering His call for uncompromising discipleship, as obligatory for my life. But then the time came when His love overwhelmed me. Then as His disciple I consciously chose His way. In the affairs of life, I tried to choose the lowly place, the way of poverty, the way of the Lamb which is described in the Sermon on the Mount. I tried not to insist upon being right, not to strike back and not to retaliate when I was wronged. During the war and the post-war period I gave up my last possessions according to Jesus' commandment: "Give and it will be given to you . . ." (Luke 6: 38). From then on I knew for myself that whoever follows Jesus is really joined to the "eternal Life", to the spring of love that flows without end. I knew that this spring of love was poured out most into the hearts of the sinful and the poor. Ever since I had begun to take seriously Jesus' call to discipleship, I was shown the real, true, divine standards for my life. Over and over again I sinned against them, but my sins drove me straight into the arms of Jesus, impelled me to claim His redeeming blood and reopened the fountain of His love.

From Jesus' visit to the home of Simon, the Pharisee, we can see how much Jesus is concerned about love that is genuine and sincere. He prizes the visible signs of Mary Magdalene's love. She ministered unto Jesus Himself; she anointed His feet with oil and kissed them. Perhaps this ointment was her most precious possession. Jesus does not yearn for "works", even though they are important and should be done through love of Him. He longs for a love that is concentrated upon Jesus Himself; it bestows gifts upon Him lavishly; it brings Him sacrifices; it is concerned about Jesus Himself.

This is the true bride, the one who says to Christ:
I do not want what is Thine, I want Thee, Thyself.
Thou art not more dear to me when I am doing well,
nor less dear when I am doing poorly.

Martin Luther

In Gethsemane, Jesus waited with such yearning in His heart for His disciples to stand by His side and show Him their love, but He sought and waited in vain. While He was in Bethany before His passion, He had also looked for love. There He found someone who sympathized with Him and understood how heavy His heart was, because the time had come for Him to begin His road of sorrows. This was Mary. Her love had shown her how deeply grieved was His soul, and she did what she could do for Him. Her entire concern was to comfort and refresh Him. That is why she did not give her money to the poor (and so incurred the disciples' reproach), but rather "wasted" it on Jesus Himself (Matt. 26: 8, 12). She wanted to comfort and refresh Him, because He was so grieved.

I shall never forget the time when it sank into my heart that because Jesus is the same today as He was yesterday, and because His heart is still suffering today, He is waiting for us to make Him happy and to refresh Him, yes—as the scriptures say—to be comforters for Him (Psalm 69: 20). Since that time my first concern has been Jesus Himself and not my ministry for Him, although I have throughout sought to fulfil that ministry. Now I was concerned about—if one may express it this way—the ministry *unto* Jesus. Since that time adoration has burned in my heart. I was grieved for Jesus' sake, because He received so little love in words and songs of adoration. Since then adoration has never been lacking in my prayer life. Although I am a pronounced active and social type, from that time on I have been constrained to spend every free minute in my room so that I could talk to Jesus in prayer. I sense that He is waiting. A bridegroom always waits for his bride to come to him so that he can carry on a dialogue of love with her.

Jesus is yearning to have fellowship with us and to hear words of love drop from our lips. He is waiting for us. He wants us to be close to Him. He wants to speak to us in our hearts, to cultivate love's intimate relationship with us. Only in times of quiet when no one else distracts us, and nothing else draws us away, can Jesus visit us with His love. Let him who wishes to know the presence of Jesus and who desires to enter into bridal love for Jesus keep his times of quiet holy and faithfully for Him.

Jesus is waiting for our love. Important as our sacrifices and our obedience to the commandments are for God (the rich young ruler sacrificed, and kept the commandments), they are not enough. Sacrifices and obedience do not necessarily yield the "eternal, divine life". Love does not necessarily pulsate through them. Jesus is pulsating life and love and He wants to impart His nature to us. Therefore, only our love, which stems from the divine, eternal life which He has granted to us, is the proper response to His love for us. This love leads us to keep His commandments, which are His wishes for us. It will lead us to bring Him many gifts, and to offer Him sacrifices—but in a different spirit.

There is something wonderful about this love for Jesus. Every bridal soul carries this love for Jesus as the most blissful secret and the most precious thing in her heart. Even if she does not speak of it, everyone who has anything to do with her senses something of this precious secret. It rests like a mysterious joy over such a soul. Radiance streams forth from her, the radiance of love. She loves Him who is the fairest of all the sons of men. She loves Him who shines through all heavens, through the whole universe like a majestic and glorious sun. She loves Him who loves her so tenderly and intimately, who loves her as no human heart possibly could, and who as the Bridegroom comes to be with her.

Yes, this love has radiant power. It radiates happiness and great joy. The Bridegroom is the Master of joy, who has been anointed with the oil of gladness above his fellows (Psalm 45: 7). His bride participates in this great joy. She belongs to Him, the Sun of love, Who shines forth in light and joy. She is united to Him in marriage. His joyful radiance falls upon her being. It is love which brings more bliss and joy than anything else into the world. The joy of an earthly bride is but a faint shadow of the true, eternal joy of the bride of the Lamb.

Bridal love for Jesus is filled with delight. There is no greater, happier, higher, richer love.

> Lord God, my Father, my strong Hero,
> In Thy Son Thou hast loved me eternally
> Before the foundation of the world.
> Thy Son hath betrothed me to Himself.
> He is my treasure; I am His bride.
> Therefore nothing can grieve me.
> Aye, aye, He will grant me heavenly life above.
> My heart shall praise Him eternally.

Philipp Nicolai (1556–1608)

Love is the Highest Calling

The only bliss which we possess on earth is loving God and knowing that He loves us.

Curé d'Ars (1785–1859)

Love—the most blissful word! God is Love; He radiates love. Heaven is love, because love is the bliss of heaven. Love, yes, love, this word resounds throughout the heavens as the sound of joy. And all the blessed and all the saints who are above love each other and they all love Jesus, the Bridegroom and the King, who is one with God the Father and the Holy Spirit.

We also may love Him. We may partake of the very nature of the Triune God—love. Through love the world was created. Through suffering love it was redeemed. Through love it will be transformed into a new heaven and a new earth. Love shines forth from every flower. Love has made creation beautiful in order to make us happy. Love fills the Father's heart and leads Him to bestow His gifts upon His earthly children in a prodigal way. It was love which made heaven into a place of never-ending happiness and blissful joy; the mansions of the Most High are for those who have loved Him.

It is love which made Jesus follow the path of martyrdom unto death in order to open the gates of heaven for us. Love impelled Him to go before us to the Father and prepare a place for us so that we might be ever near Him, the eternal Love. Love wants to bring us to the supreme happiness for which we were created. It wants to bring us into the unity of love with God; this unity alone can make us truly happy.

Love, bridal love! Who can comprehend its secret? Its depth and its height, its length and its breadth are incomprehensible! For bridal love reveals the heart of Jesus Himself, the heart of the Bridegroom, which pulsates for a sinful

27

human being as for His bride. He embraces her in intimate love. He is concerned for her smallest needs and cares, and bears them with her. As her Protector and Helper, He is always at her side. He ennobles and adorns her, like a bridegroom who cares for his bride so that she might be beautiful, as He is.

Who is like the Bridegroom of eternal love! He could not keep this love to Himself. He created man and called him to love Him. He alone is the Happiness of true love. He alone can grant us ultimate fulfilment. His love imbues us with delight. His love will never disappoint us. He is a royal Lord; nevertheless we sinners are betrothed to Him as His bride. He is the Ruler of the universe; yet we are permitted to love Him. One day we shall rule the universe in the unity of His love.

We may love the fairest of the sons of men who bears the stigmata as a sign of His most perfect love. We may love the Man of Sorrows whose love streamed forth in immeasurable suffering for our redemption. He did not count the cost of this suffering. In Gethsemane His soul almost died from the hellish torture; He sweated blood, and His countenance was disfigured by agony and terror. When they scourged Him His whole body was covered with wounds. He suffered unspeakably. He was despised and rejected—He who was the Son of God, whom all the angels served, through whom we were created! He was trampled under foot by hatred, scorn and slander. He was pierced by the arrows of hate of those to whom He had brought only love, help and healing, and the news of the Kingdom of Heaven. All of this He suffered out of love. Who can fathom such love?

We may love Him who bore His cross so quietly and patiently. He took upon Himself all our burdens. He suffered Himself to be nailed to the cross in dreadful agony. Tortured to death, He gave His life on that cross so that His blood, flowing down upon this dark, sinful, satanic earth might redeem those who claim in faith the power of the blood. We may love the victorious risen Lord who revealed the triumph of love over death and hell and who brings everyone who loves Him to partake of His resurrected life.

Whom shall we love?—Him who contains all love in Himself—who is most worthy of love in heaven and earth. Incomprehensibly, He loves us. We were created and redeemed for this love. Blessed is he who hears Him ask: "Do you love me?" and answers: "Lord You know everything; You know that I love You."

The Royal Offer

There is One who walks up and down the streets, in and out of the houses. He has something to offer. What is it? It is His love. Everyone He meets, He stops and asks: "Will you take what I have to offer? It is my love. You are seeking something to make you happy. You would give good money for it, expend your time and energy. I am offering you My love. In it you will find everything you are looking for and everything that could make you happy. Believe Me! Accept it!"

Those, to whom He speaks, answer: "What do we have to do for this?" He says: "Make room so that My love can pour in. My gift of love cannot be compared with anything else, neither with a person nor with an object that could be loved. The one condition is that you make room for it. I can not make this gift to a heart which is already filled; there would be no room for it. I am seeking untenanted hearts. Cast out everything that fills your heart and you will gain the most precious object in the world: the closest, the most intimate, the holiest and strongest bond of love between us. Yes, deny all else, and you will find it!"

Whoever accepts in faith this royal offer of love, whoever opens his heart to Jesus and dedicates himself to Him, yes, whoever becomes His dearest bride, will discover that He is the One, the great Love. Jesus offers us the supreme gift!

Loving Jesus means
*   to have and to hold for one's own*
*   the greatest treasure of earth and heaven.*
Loving Jesus means
*   to lavish on Him the offering of oneself.*

Jesus is Love everlasting;
He came to us below,
That God to all His children
His wondrous love might show.

Jesus's love was so boundless
That many then were moved
To give themselves to loving;
Because of Him they loved.

Jesus with love still is seeking
For hearts that are aflame
To make their lives an offering.
Inspired by love for Him.

Love that's eternal is waiting
And pleads with every heart,
"O, won't you hear and answer?
'Tis pain to dwell apart."

* WJ 225

* Basilea Schlink, *Well-spring of Joy*, Songs of the Sisters of Mary for Singing or Praying; subsequent extracts are similarly indicated.

Jesus — A True Bridegroom

Jesus is a true Bridegroom; this is His very nature. That is why He calls Himself Bridegroom in the Scriptures. His great love desires a bride, a bridal soul. He longs fervently for her love. He looks for her to see whether she is about to come to Him, to see whether she longs and yearns for Him, to see whether she really wants Him alone.

Jesus is a true Bridegroom; this is His very nature. He wants to give us His love; but He is also waiting for us to return His love. Jesus is a true Bridegroom. His love is a jealous love. He wants you, your soul, completely. He is jealous when you give your love to other people and other things. He is jealous when you pay more attention to them, when you give them more time, more of yourself, than you give Him. Then He stands beside you, grieved. Then He is hurt and wounded, because He loves you so much.

Jesus is a true Bridegroom. He does not force you to love Him. He asks: "Will you give Me your love?", and He gets what He wants when you do this. Only one thing will satisfy Him—your love. All else is too small for Him: that you believe in Him, that you obey Him, that you come to Him for forgiveness. He is not only your Physician who heals you. He is not only your Redeemer who delivers you from your bonds. He wants to be your Bridegroom, and as Bridegroom He gives you His great, His tender, His most intimate love. Now He is waiting for you to give Him your love. He who loves wants to be loved in return.

Because Jesus is the Bridegroom, He can be wounded if you take up self-chosen crosses, choose the way of poverty and resolve to make sacrifices simply for ascetic reasons. Certainly He wants you to follow Him on the way of the cross. But His heart is filled with grief and sorrow if it is not love that impels you. You should not take the way of the cross for your own sanctification, but rather—as He repeatedly said while He was on earth—"*For My sake* you should lose your life, *for My sake* you should forsake houses, brethren . . .' Out of love for Him, out of love alone you should choose poverty, obedience, lowliness, humility and disgrace. Only the dedication which springs from love will make Him happy. Indeed, this is the only dedication which He will accept. Nothing else. All else is insufficient. Anything else would be more likely to wound Him, because it is simply pious deceit; we seem to be going His way, but it is really for our own sake. So He poses the question: "Do you really love Me? If you give Me your love, you give Me all that I desire!"

Jesus, the Bridegroom, is the Man of Sorrows. He suffers to this present day. He is seeking a bride who will share with Him what is in His heart. His heart is filled not only with love, but also with suffering—past and present. He is seeking a bride who will really live out the bridal state, whose heart will beat with His, who will bear things with Him, who not only suffers through her own afflictions, but also suffers His afflictions with Him, who in reality enters into the fellowship of suffering with Him. Only she is a true bride who is concerned about His concerns—about the needs of His people and His church and the things which hinder His dominion among the peoples.

For Him the bride is the soul who suffers with Him and who is prepared to do everything to alleviate His sufferings. She seeks ways through sacrifice and prayer and does her utmost to ensure that the things which trouble Him may be changed. She labours so that He may be honoured where He is not now honoured, that He may be loved where He is not now loved, that He may be feared where He is not now feared. She strives to lead back to God the people who are not living according to His commandments and statutes, and so she comforts His heart and makes Him happy. She loves, spends her life for Him and suffers until she has loved souls home to Him by whom they can be saved, until people set

33

themselves under His dominion and begin to love Him. Not until her Bridegroom is comforted will she be satisfied. The bride keeps asking Him: "How can I comfort You?", and in the quietness the Bridegroom will tell her what grieves Him. She will go with Him to comfort Him.

Jesus is a true Bridegroom; this is His very nature. That is why He is not satisfied when we simply set ourselves under His dominion and give Him slavish obedience. He wants more—He wants our heart, our very heart's blood. As the Bridegroom, He asks: "How much am I worth to you? How much can you sacrifice for Me? Can you give Me your beloved children? Can you give Me father and mother and friends? Can you give Me your home and your native land out of love if I ask for these? Will you go anywhere I call you to serve, and lead to Me the souls for which I hunger? Can you sacrifice your honour, your strength, your longing to be loved, your deepest secret wishes for Me?"

Jesus is a true Bridegroom; this is His very nature. He waits for His bride. He does not seek to force love; it must be spontaneous. He knocks softly on the door. He waits until someone opens it. He stands behind the door and looks to see whether His bride will open up and come out to Him (Song of Solomon 5: 2). His eyes follow her sadly if all day long she is busy and in a hurry, if she goes about everything quickly and vigorously and yet spiritually is becoming estranged from Him, because she is completely engrossed with her work and earthly business.

Jesus is a true Bridegroom; this is His very nature. His ardent concern is to impart His likeness to His bride so that she too may radiate divine beauty and be adorned with many virtues. He works with special care, loving care for His bride. He guides her and leads her along paths of chastisement, for this will bring her to where He is. He dreams of the full beauty that shall be hers. He loves her too much to suffer her to have any "spots" or "wrinkles", because she is His bride. Full of pride and joy, His loving eye beholds her as though she were perfect. Through the power of His blood

He, the Almighty, can bring her to the perfection of divine beauty.

Jesus is a true Bridegroom; this is His very nature. So He stands as a Protector beside His bride. He is intent upon protecting her from all who may want to harm her. He strives on her behalf. To be a bride means that one is no longer alone. It means that one has an intimate partner who lives for his bride, and to do everything that he can for her. So, Jesus, the Bridegroom, lives to do everything for His bride, to help her in every situation, in every need, in every impossibility. She is no longer alone. Jesus is a true Bridegroom; this is His very nature. He is waiting in heaven for the day when His bride will come to Him so that He can be united with her for ever. He seeks her in unending love.

I will betroth you to Me forever;
I will betroth you to Me in righteous and in justice,
In steadfast love, and in mercy.
I will betroth you to Me in faithfulness;
And you shall know the Lord.

Hosea 2: 19, 20

Sweetest Jesus, Spouse divine,
Whose is greater worth than Thine
To be loved and honoured.

Thou my Sun, whose radiant beams
Through my heart in glory stream
From Thy love so holy.

Joy Thou bringest to my heart,
Balm in suffering dost impart,
Thou art ever loving.

Who could ever happier be
Than the bride, beloved by Thee,
To Thy love responding?

She rejoices, thrills and glows,
Sings for joy because she knows
She is so beloved.

WJ 223

Who Will Attain the Treasure of Bridal Love?

We find the bridal love for Jesus when we respond to His love. He, the Bridegroom, stands before the door of our heart and knocks. It is heart-moving and virtually inconceivable that He whom the whole heaven, all seraphim and cherubim bring honour without end is not satisfied with this adoration, but rather desires something else—your love and my love. It is incomprehensible that Jesus should humble Himself and draw nigh to us, that He should stand at the door of our heart like a beggar for love and entreat us: "Give Me your love!" Do we realize how often He repeats this request—full of longing for us?

O love of God most holy,
You came from God's own heart,
As Beggar meek and lowly
To ev'ry human heart.
Beyond man's understanding
Is such humility,
God begging men to love Him!
What will our answer be?

Alas, alas, too often
Your begging is in vain.
Your love beyond man's measure
Is treated with disdain.
Along Your way of anguish
The angels weep above
But who else heeds Your pleading,
O Beggar for man's love?

From soul to soul You wander,
You knock at ev'ry door.
You long to be united
With men for evermore.
As Spouse, Your bride You proffer
A love reserved for her,
But men reject Your offer,
Their worldly loves prefer.

Accept us then, O Bridegroom,
We give You all our heart
To quench the ceaseless longing
Of Your love-hungry heart.
O make in us Your dwelling,
So that alone with You,
The fire of love may kindle
Uniting us with You.

BELIEVE HIS OFFER OF LOVE

If I wish to find and attain bridal love, the first thing I must do is believe that Jesus is standing before the door of my heart seeking admission. I must believe that He is concerned about my love. Jesus is standing before us, asking us a question (it is actually the only question which really concerns Him): "Do you love Me?"

In this question lies Jesus' desire to be loved. He is asking for our love. It is precious to Him. It is the thing He desires most. This is the first question He asked Peter after His resurrection. It is the question of the risen Lord to all of us who know how He suffered and died for us out of love: "Will you respond to My love by giving Me yours? Will you give Me your heart, so that there is nothing else in it but Me alone? Do you love Me?"

Whoever cannot believe that Jesus' greatest desire is for our love, should learn that God's first commandment is to love Him above everything else.

> You shall love the Lord your God
> With all your heart, and with all your soul
> And with all your mind.

> Matt. 22: 37

Whoever still cannot believe it, may he hear the lamentations from the heart of God over His bride Israel, because her love is like a morning cloud (Hos. 6: 4) and because she keeps forgetting Him, even though He is her husband. Great was God's lamentation, because she continually gave her love to other things—to people and transient things—and did not, like a bride, give God her first love; God who had made a covenant of love with her. How precious our love must be to Him if He laments so much because He does not receive it!

"I have loved you with an everlasting love" (Jer. 31: 3)—

yes, hear: "I love you", says the Lord. We must listen to this voice. Oh, if we only believed it! For Jesus it is too small a thing to have redeemed us, to have freed us from the bonds of the devil. He wants to give us more. He wants to enter into a covenant of love with us for time and eternity. His love urges us to be united with Him, to be in Him, to share everything with Him.

> When I passed by you again and looked upon you, behold, you were at the age for love; and I spread my skirt over you, and covered your nakedness: Yea, I plighted my troth to you and entered into a covenant with you, says the Lord God, and you became mine.

Ezekiel 16: 8

Whoever finds it difficult to believe that Jesus loves us so intimately, that He loves us as a bridegroom loves his bride, his doubts must be overcome when he hears the pledge of the Word of God that those who love Him and His appearing will be crowned (2 Tim. 4: 8) and will sit with Him upon His throne as conquerors (Rev. 3: 21). I prove my love for a person if I always desire to have him at my side. Jesus loves His bride so very much that He will take her up to Himself to His throne. He wants to have His bride with Him at all times.

That overwhelmed me so much that I dedicated my whole life to Jesus as His bride. It was incomprehensible to me: He wants to do everything together with me. He will do nothing without me. He wants to rule the universe and judge the peoples together with His bride. That is why He will arrange a wedding celebration for her. How could God call the great festival of heaven a wedding—which means a union of love—if Jesus were not the Bridegroom, and if His bride, the bride of the Lamb, did not consist of only bridal souls, who had a passionate love for Jesus? The union of love with Jesus has to be a complete love.

Yes, because His love is so desirous of being united with our soul, it is true: He stands before the door of my heart and asks for my love. Now it is my task to accept Him into my heart, if I want to attain bridal love. I must dedicate myself to Him—by word of mouth, but preferably in writing. On earth it is not sufficient if a man tells a woman that he loves her. She has to return this love. She has to dedicate her life to him; otherwise she is not really a bride. And so Jesus stands before you asking and waiting for your love. Not until you answer will the blissful stream of His love flow into your heart. His love is divine life, and it streams into our heart only in so far as we dedicate ourselves to Jesus.

My Jesus,
I will myself to Thee,
my intimate Saviour and Bridegroom,
Christ Jesus,
to be Thy complete and eternal possession.
I renounce with my heart all rights
and power,
which Satan may have over me,
from this evening on;
from this Maundy Thursday evening when
Thou, my Bridegroom in blood,
hast purchased me for Thine own bride,
hast burst the gates of hell and
hast lovingly opened
the heart of Thy Father for me
through Thy battle of death, wrestling
and sweating blood in the Garden of Gethsemane.
From this evening on
may my heart and all my love
out of indebted gratitude for ever more
be yielded and devoted to Thee.
From now on into eternity
may not my will
but Thine be done!

Command, rule and reign in me!
I grant Thee authority over me
and promise
with Thy support and assistance,
I would rather let the last drop of my blood be shed
than with will and knowledge
inwardly or outwardly,
become unfaithful or disobedient to Thee.
Behold, Thou hast me completely,
sweet Friend of my soul.
In chaste, virgin love
I will always remain faithful to Thee.
May Thy Spirit not depart from me,
and may Thy battle of death support me!
Yea, Amen! May Thy Spirit affix His seal
to that which I have written in childlike sincerity!
Thine unworthy possession . . .

Gerhard Tersteegen (1697—1769)

Love for Jesus is the commitment which can say: Take my life and everything that makes life worth living for me—people, goods and wishes of all sorts. I love You. That is why I have to give You everything. Love holds nothing back. Yes, it wants to give the Beloved those things which are especially valuable. A genuine lover would not be satisfied with less.

How can we comprehend that what Jesus desires from us is actually such a simple thing—just to love Him? How can we understand that He wants something so beautiful and so blissful—not just obedience, but rather fervent love? He leads us to do what makes us happiest—love. This is not just a relationship with some human being, who may disappoint us, and with whom the relationship of love may be quickly dimmed. No, we may love Him who will never disappoint us and who loves us with an inexpressible love.

There is no love perfectly joyful
aside from that
with which a man loves God—
and no faithfulness completely blest
aside from that
which joins a man to Christ.

Søren Kierkegaard (1813–1855)

Jesus stands humbly before the door of our heart and knocks; yet He, God and King, knows His worth and knows what He is offering when He offers us His love, the greatest blessing for time and eternity, the highest gift that a man can seek and attain. That is why Jesus gives us these commandments: "Whoever of you does not renounce all that he has . . ." (Luke 14: 33)—"He who loves father or mother more than Me is not worthy of Me" (Matt. 10: 37)—"If any one . . . does not hate his own father and mother . . . and even his own life, he cannot be My disciple" (Luke 14: 26).

Jesus speaks these words in His royal dignity as a Lover. He does not utter them primarily as a Teacher, nor as a Lord who demands obedience. He says these words as Bridegroom. In the Psalm which is concerned with the relationship between bride and bridegroom, the Lord speaks: "Hear, O daughter, consider, and incline your ear; forget your people and your father's house; and the king will desire your beauty . . ." (Psalm 45: 10, 11). The Bridegroom calls the bride to forget everything, to leave everything behind for Him, so that He can delight in her.

Jesus' pressing question is always this: Who is more loved—He or our ego, people and things? That is why Jesus always begins His invitation with "For My sake . . ." This invitation to relinquish everything else for His sake is possible only for the soul who loves in a bridal manner. For a bride it is a foregone conclusion that the Bridegroom commands: "Leave your home, your occupation, now leave your native land. Come with Me!" For those who are not brides these words often prove an offence and an annoyance; but love, however, wants to give all and to sacrifice for the Beloved. For love the element of life is sacrifice.

Jesus as the loving Bridegroom has the right to ask: "Will you give up everything for Me? Will you forsake everything

for Me? Will you yearn for nothing more than to ga.....
love and My pleasure? Are you prepared to give up earth.
precious things in order to gain the most precious—Me and
My love? Am I worth so much to you that you would give
up everything for My love? Is it worth more to you than the
love of people? Do you love Me? Do you love Me more than
anything else?"

"Do you love Me?" asks Jesus. "Only if you love Me more
than anything else will you come to know My love. I do not
waste it on those who only give Me a little love, who give
Me only a divided love. I do not reveal My heart to them. I
do not pour out My love and the benefits of My love—even
earthly gifts—over them. They will not come to know how I
repay a hundredfold what they gave Me. They will not gain
anything; they will be satisfied neither with earthly love and
gifts, nor with My love and My gifts. I cannot fully bestow
on them My love and My gifts. I will only reveal myself
to him who really loves Me. His whole heart will be filled
with heavenly bliss—even in the midst of suffering—because I, the King of heaven, Love itself, have come to dwell
in him."

Consider, therefore, what you are missing, both in time
and in eternity, if you love Jesus with only half a heart—you
are missing the greatest blessing which is offered to man.
There will be no other opportunity. Only those who have
loved Jesus here with bridal love, with the first love, will be
able to share in the marriage supper of the Lamb, in the
great union of love between Jesus and the bridal souls, in the
hour of bliss which all heaven has been living for.

If you want to know the Bridegroom who is knocking at
your door, then forsake beloved ones to receive the most
Beloved, the most dear One, Jesus! Hear His constant plea: "I
want you utterly!"—Deliver everything up to Him—even
every feeling or thought that centres on people, on all
earthly and created things apart from Him. Jesus is waiting
to receive our undivided love. He is waiting for us to yield to
Him all our feelings, thoughts and desires. He prodigally

bestows His gifts upon those who love Him above every-thing else. He loves them beyond measure.

The most wondrous, the most blissful state in heaven and earth—to know Him and His love—does not fall into a person's lap by chance, but it is the reward of everyone who gives everything to Jesus. Every longing of his heart is then directed towards Jesus. Every impulse of the will flows into His will. The whole existence of the bride is dominated by His word: "You have I chosen. You only!" Jesus does not divide His love. Therefore, gladly do everything needful that you may know this most powerful, most blissful love, the love of Jesus. Is it not seemly that Jesus, whose love is like a fiery sun, like a powerful magnet, should take us entirely into His possession, and that we should forsake all else for Him? Truly this is so! Let us ask Him to make us His brides. This is the plea that Jesus is waiting for, and He will fulfil it.

If you wish to have Jesus completely,
give yourself to Him completely.
If you wish to be loved full-heartedly by Him,
love Him full-heartedly.

O make me Thine,
My Saviour, Lord most holy,
That I may only
Live to give Thee glory,
O make me Thine.

O make me Thine—
Thou art my life and treasure,
In Thee alone
My heart finds joy and pleasure,
O make me Thine!

O make me Thine,
For Thou to me hast given
Thyself, and so
My heart leaps up to heaven,
Loves Thee alone.

O make me thine—
Take all I love and treasure,
My life, my honour—
If that brings Thee pleasure
And shows my love—
Yes, make them Thine!

WJ 227

THE INFALLIBLE WAY

Her sins, which are many, are forgiven, for she loved much.

Luke 7: 47

A woman comes to Jesus. Her heart is so burdened by reason of her sin that she falls at Jesus' feet and can only cry. Her heart is filled with sorrow and anguish because of what she has done; she is overwhelmed by her guilt towards God and man. One who can cry over his sins—one who loves Jesus greatly! Is there a connection? This is the woman of whom Jesus said: "She loved much." Yes, she proved her love for Jesus. She did what the Pharisee, the host, had neglected to do. She showed Him her love. That is why Jesus asks him: "Which of them (the debtors) will love him more?"—and the Pharisee himself gave the answer: "The one, I suppose, to whom he forgave more."

The forgiveness of sins is the true source of bridal love. Thousands know Jesus as their Redeemer, but they do not feel a personal love for Him. This woman's tears and contrite heart brought her to love. Her sins drove her to Jesus. Her grieving heart opened her eyes, not only to see her sin but to see Jesus Himself. She saw how beautiful He is and how worthy of love He is. Hearts which mourn for their sins, beg forgiveness and attain it, are ready for Him, and Jesus can pour His love into them. Then it streams powerfully back to Him. Just as this woman had previously loved the world, herself and her lust, so now she was led to abhor these things, to weep for them and to love Him.

This woman cannot sufficiently express her love for Jesus. She anoints His head. She washes His feet. The host had neglected this expression of love, which was normally performed for every guest who entered a house after wandering through the hot sand. But this woman washed His feet, because her love constrained her—not with water, which she could easily have drawn and which would have cost her

48

nothing, but rather with her own tears. She poured out her heart in these tears of repentance and gratitude for forgiveness. Every sorrowful repentant tear was an expression of her love for Jesus.

We can see from Jesus' words how deeply His heart was moved by such a "foot-washing". He had never known one like this before. It refreshed and rejoiced His heart. There is joy in heaven over every sinner who repents, but there is even more joy over a sinner who does a good deed for Jesus with a loving, penitent heart.

Yet, this woman does even more. A special, intimate proof of love among human beings is the kiss, and she cannot help but kiss the feet of Jesus. Her heart is gripped by Him who loves her, who has forgiven her, who came to earth to save her from all her sins, to give her salvation and to call her to His side. She was probably one of the women who followed Him around the countryside while He was on earth, and above she will be at His side for all eternity.

Her love was intended for Jesus personally. She was concerned with Jesus Himself. She was not primarily concerned with the fact that He had obliterated her guilt. No, her heart was kindled with a personal love for Him. She had to do something for Him. She gave Him the thing which His heart most deeply desires: love in response to His unspeakable love.

That is why Jesus writes her a testimonial: "She loved much"—the highest praise He can give—because here it is a question of love for Him. She loved Him much. She showed Him love, and this love flowed from her repentance. All this is true for us. Love for Jesus can flow only from a heart that can mourn over its sin and guilt. Daily we sin against God and man, and daily our Lord looks to us to repent. In this repentance we may show our love, let it stream forth to Him and be acceptable in His sight every day.

So if we would attain to bridal love and cultivate it, our urgent plea must be: "Show me ever anew that I am a great sinner before God and man: Grant me ever anew a contrite heart like this woman's. Grant me ever anew a heart that can weep over my sins so that I can cast myself at the feet of Jesus and at the feet of those I have hurt or wronged. Do not let me shrink from the pain which it brings to recognize my sins, to confess them and suffer for them ever anew—only in this manner can You grant me the grace of the tears which are proof of my love for You!"

He will hear such pleas. What does His heart long for more than this love which is born out of repentance? Therefore, a fountain of love will spring up in our hearts and Jesus will have a bride who loves Him beyond all else and who seeks every possible way to please Him.

The grace of repentance does not only make it possible for us to love, but it also prepares us for the fellowship of His sufferings. Peter proved this. He said to the risen Lord: "You know everything; You know that I love You."—What a wonderful assurance! Peter could say with all his heart: "You search all things, You know what is happening in the whole universe; You know every heart and what is in it—You know that my heart is consumed with love for You, Jesus." Yes, Peter can say that in spite of the fact that he had denied Jesus and ought to have confessed his lack of love. He cannot but say what he does. From his great sin of denial sprang the tears of repentance, and those tears enhanced his sight so that he could see Jesus as He is: as the Man of Sorrows, filled with endless love, who can still lovingly behold those who tortured Him.

> *Lord Jesus, look on me, I pray*
> *As once on Peter Thou didst gaze,*
> *That I may learn repentance.*
> *Jesus, Thy glance great wonders wrought,*
> *Peter to penitence it brought,*
> *May it to me be granted.*
>
> *Jesus, my sinning wounds Thy heart,*
> *To Thee I pain on pain impart,*

How blind I am and heedless!
Therefore, O Jesus, look on me,
That what through sin I do to Thee
I may with shame acknowledge.

O look on me, so let me see
How sad Thy heart because of me,
Then will my heart start mourning.
I beg of Thee, grant me to see
Thy look of grief; Lord, come to me,
Make me repent my sinning.

Because this happened to Peter, his heart was seized by such love that he had to cry: 'I love Thee. I cannot do anything but love Thee. My heart and my whole being, everything that I am and have—all I can do is give it to Thee.' And Peter made good his word in all that followed.

That is the mark of the great love which is born of repentance. It wants to be with Him whom it loves, no matter what it costs. It even longs to tread the path of sufferings. It aspires never to forsake Him.

The Secret of Seeking

WHERE IS HE WHOM MY SOUL LOVES?

Whoever has discovered the precious secret of bridal love for Jesus, whoever has tasted the happiness of having found Jesus, will time and again discover that it is also possible to "lose" Him. The Holy Scriptures show us Shulammite wandering through the streets at night seeking the one she loves (Song of Solomon 1: 7; 3: 1, 2), because suddenly he is no longer with her. For the soul burning with love this separation is the greatest agony. This soul knows: He is the only One who can make me happy. It knows and feels: If I have everything else on earth that I desire but have Him not, the pearl of my life is missing. Only One can love me so much that my soul receives the fulness of love that it desires. If He is not with me, I wander lonely at night in desert places. When I come home, there will be no one there. Only my Bridegroom would have awaited me.

The loving soul knows: If my heart is filled with cares and misery, I cannot find anyone anywhere who could take these burdens from me except my Bridegroom. He is strong and has an eye of love, which discerns immediately what the burden is that is weighing so heavily upon me. He takes it upon His back. He can bear the load. The loving soul knows: If I have lost Him, I have no one else to whom I could turn. I have no one else who understands the very depths within me. He is the only one who can do this. He knows and understands me, because He created me Himself. He discerns with His loving eye the most subtle things in my heart. He knows what makes my heart mourn and what it longs for. He sees and understands. He alone can help me.

So the bride of Jesus confesses: I must have Him. There is

nothing else that I need. He can fill my life wholly and completely. My soul was created for Him. Therefore, I can receive the things I desire only from my Lord and Bridegroom. Without Him I cannot exist. If I lose Him—through my sin, through my indifference, by going my own way—then it is as though my life had come to an end. I am like a burned-out volcano. I no longer have the One who alone can make me happy through His love. The joy of my life has disappeared. He alone can cause joy to flow into my heart so that I am not vulnerable to all the suffering which may come upon me. If I lose Him, I am the most pitiable of all the sons of men. Then I am defenceless before all the temptations which fall upon my soul. My Bridegroom who would stand by me, defend me and protect me from all attacks of the enemy is no longer there. Now I no longer have anyone on whom I can lean when I am weak. What hope is there for me now? He could do for me what in my weakness I cannot do.

The bride of Jesus knows: Without Him I cannot do anything that would contain blessing, that would be fruitful, that would make others happy. I am poverty-stricken, if I lose Him. Without Him I can no longer live.

What should the soul do in its great affliction? Like Shulammite, it will arise and seek Jesus, its Bridegroom. So long as we are on the earth we may often have the same experience as Shulammite had. We lose Him when we do not dedicate our will. We lose Him when we are engrossed with other things—with our work, other people, our honour, our self-satisfaction. We lose Him when we give way to our sinful inclinations instead of bringing them to Him and letting ourselves be cleansed from our sins through His blood. To lose Him is the most terrible thing that can happen to us. Without Him we are like chaff which is blown away in the wind. Without Him we are helpless before the powers and forces which threaten us on all sides. That is why we need our Lord Jesus Christ as the loving Bridegroom.

Where do we find Him whom our soul loves? Where can I be sure to find Him always?

At certain places which are landmarks along His way. Bridal love means to be there where the Bridegroom is. Jesus does not recognize any other type of love as bridal love. No matter how much we seek Him, we shall never find Him if we do not look in the places where alone He is to be found.

Where I am, there shall My Servant be also.
John 12: 26

Jesus abides still in those places where He was to be found when on the earth. These places are still the same. They are the places of humiliation and abasement, of surrendering, sacrificing and suffering. Allegorically speaking, we can hurry through all the streets and squares like Shulammite and still not find Him, simply because we are not looking where He is. That place does not please us. If a bride tells her bridegroom that she loves him, she proves her love by wanting to be where he is. If his duty lies in some foreign land or in some place which she would otherwise dislike, she shows her love by following him. She wants to be with him whatever it costs.

If we will look for Jesus where He is we shall have Him for our Bridegroom. Then He will give us His bliss, His help, His power, His strength—everything we need and all the ineffable, wonderful things which are His. No one can declare that he loves Jesus, that he is Jesus' bride, without longing to be with Him. The moment a bride is aware that she no longer wants to be with her bridegroom, she has broken the relationship of love. She ceases to be His bride; there has been a separation.

Very quickly it can come to a divorce. Earthly divorces are also but a reflex of what can take place between a human soul and the heavenly Bridegroom. There is such divorce the moment we no longer want to be where Jesus is. True bridal love can only become deeper and more intense as we entirely desire to go with Him on His way of humiliation, of surrender and sacrifice, and to be with Him in the places that spell suffering and death for our ego.

Where You go I will go and where You lodge I will lodge . . .
Where You die I will die, and there will I be buried.

Ruth 1: 16, 17

Let me, Lord, go along with You
Both joy and sorrow share with You,
Close at Your side for ever.

O let me stand close by Your side,
Your sufferings share with joy and pride
For those You have redeemed.

O let me be a bride of Yours
Choose not my will, but only Yours,
I yearn to give You pleasure.

Let me become like Thee quite small.
You came, Lord, who created all
From heaven to a stable.

WJ 228

THE MAN OF SORROWS TODAY

Jesus, our Bridegroom—where do we find Him? Let us ask ourselves: what was the sign of His love two thousand years ago? His passion! It is the same today—the sufferings of Jesus continue right down to this day. Just as it was the sin of man which caused Jesus to go the agonizing way of His passion then, so today the sin of man causes Him to suffer—for still He lives and loves. Whenever those who belong to Him are ridiculed, expelled, judged, He suffers also, because He lives in them. That is why the places where one is certain to find Jesus are the same places where the disciples also could have found Him. The disciples could have found Jesus; they could have come into the unity of love with Him if they had watched with Him in Gethsemane. But they fell asleep, and left Him alone. That is why they lost Him. That is why they fell into hopelessness and despair.

So I too can only find Him whom my soul loves when I am willing to tarry in "Gethsemane", the place where everything around me crumbles to pieces, where I am in distress and temptation: "Where is now my God?" I find Him when my heart bleeds (as Jesus sweated blood in Gethsemane) and can still say: "My Father, Thy will be done!"—even when I am tortured, under the attack of the powers of darkness. For Jesus, Gethsemane was the final preparation for His death on the cross. So we also shall be tempted by evil spirits (as we see in Ephesians 6); these temptations are part of our lot. Whenever we are willing to surrender our will completely and to suffer these temptations, we are being prepared so that we may really be crucified with Jesus (Rom. 6).

When have we found our Bridegroom? We have found Him when these temptations have driven us to His side and we can say:

> *My Jesus, here will I kneel beside Thee*
> *At this rock of Thy fear and agony.*

Out of love will I stay with Thee,
When Thou leadest me through the dark valley.
I will stay by Thee.
*I will endure to the end with Thee.**

The disciples could have found Jesus as He was led through the valley of Kidron on the way to the house of the high priest. But they were not with Him. They had fled. That is why they were in need and despair. If they had stayed by Jesus and had let themselves be bound also, they would have experienced His power, His sustenance, His peace and something of His glory. But they went astray; they followed other paths. Their hearts were tortured and there was no peace in their souls.

Jesus stood where He was taken prisoner and said: "Here am I", that is, Take Me, guards, bind Me and lead Me, wherever you will; all this is happening with My Father's consent. If we want to find Him today and to be with Him, we must let ourselves be bound to the place or to the job which, it may be, we do not care for at all. He who lets himself be taken prisoner and gives up his freedom, instead of following his own desires has fellowship with Jesus.

Where is He whom we love? Where should we expect to find Him? He stands before His judges. His disciples were not to be seen there—the disciples who perhaps could have testified on His behalf. Instead, they were filled with despair; it seemed as if all their longings and hopes had been dashed to pieces. Their Master had been taken prisoner! He stood before the judges! Why did they despair? Because they were not where their Lord and Bridegroom was.

Whoever lets himself be led before the tribunal will find the Bridegroom. There He is sure to be. Today Jesus is always present at the place of judgment. How simple it would be for us to find Him! Instead we lament and say: 'He is so far away—He is no longer with us . . .'' Let us ask

* Text of the Gethsemane plaque in the Garden of Jesus' Suffering.

ourselves: When He stands before the judges are we there with Him? Are we to be accused? Unjustly accused? The disciples were not ready, and that is why they were unhappy. They deserved to lose Jesus.

If we would only let others show us where we have gone wrong! Our loss of Jesus begins in the smallest things. We lose the Bridegroom whenever we will not suffer others to correct us, to show us what we have neglected to do or what we have done wrong. Jesus is to be found at the place where He let Himself be accused before the judges. If the bride stood there also, she would immediately be with Him. She would be united with Him; and even while she is being convicted, she would know the taste of heaven.

We draw closer to Him as we stay silent when we are accused. We must behave exactly as He did. Jesus remained silent when people reproached Him, although He was innocent: how much more should that be our reaction, for after all we are the guilty ones! If we do not accept justified reproach, we sunder the relationship of bridal love to Jesus and join ourselves to Satan, the rebel who has always refused to accept correction and who angrily protests against it.

So we know now where we can find Jesus. As He stood before His judges then, so He stands today as the One who is accused by millions. At that earlier judgment He did not find a single defender among the countless people for whom He had sacrificed Himself, whom He had healed and to whom He had done good. In that hour no one appeared to press through the mob to speak a word on His behalf. If we want to be with Jesus, we should not expect any human help when we suffer injustice or when we are wrongly accused. It is just then that we are close to Him.

It is at the place of judgment that we have the best opportunity to find Jesus, because that is where He spent most of His time. He was dragged before four judges. Accusations caused Him the deepest pain; they even assailed Him on the cross, where men still falsely accused Him. The place of judgment plunged Jesus in the deepest suffering. If we do not want to stand in the place where He suffered so much, we shall lose Him. We must seek Him and seek Him until we repent and He can join us to Himself again.

Yet if we cannot bear to be told the truth—which is no great ordeal—and admit our faults, how can we possibly stand at the place where He was scourged or at the place where He was crowned with a crown of thorns?

There it is not simply a matter of being wrongly accused; rather, it is a matter of being tortured, of being disgraced and slandered, of being ridiculed and derided and thought to be odd. Jesus is still to be found at the place where He was crowned with a crown of thorns. We can find Him there today. It is in ridicule and disgrace that we are united with Him in love, in a unity more real than we could know in all the uplifting spiritual experiences which He could grant us.

We do often wait in vain for "beautiful experiences"! But we should rather go to the place where we can find unity with Him as we participate in real experience. Blessings, even the gift of bridal love, are only to be gained when the foundation has been laid through judgment. If one removes this foundation, one is in danger of living in a dream world or becoming a hypocrite, and we are no longer treading the path of Jesus. Although we may still presume to say that we belong to Jesus and that we are as close to Him as a bride, we are in reality very far from Him.

But if we go to the place of suffering, if we endure pain, misery and sickness, He joins Himself to us, and love's glory begins to shine. We find Jesus on the way of the cross, when such a heavy burden is placed upon our shoulders that we feel that we can no longer stand erect. If various burdens seem to weigh us down to the ground and the Lord still continues to heap fresh burdens upon us, then we may know that He is near us, and we are joined to Him: we receive all the love and help, the comfort, the most tender understanding, sympathy, refreshment, heavenly joy and other gifts that are His.

We can even come to the point where we actually choose crucifixion, allowing everything to be nailed to the cross—things which we would normally desire to preserve, but which God's judgments have sentenced to death. When we dedicate ourselves to this course, we are united with our Bridegroom, and we bear the signs of the Bridegroom: the wounds. The path of Jesus was marked by wounds. Even at the first station He was wounded in His soul. At the scourging His wounds were countless. Their number increased when He was crowned with a crown of thorns and again when He bore His cross up to Golgotha where the nails pierced His hands and feet.

It may be that at certain times of our life Jesus calls us to a particular station of His passion where He wills to have us at His side. It is only when we let ourselves be wounded— and because of our sins suffer some small degree of affliction—that He will recognize us as His true bride. Therefore, we should rejoice over the wounds which our soul and spirit bear. Let us rejoice over our bodily sufferings, because then we are close to the Lord Jesus as His bride. Peace streams into our heart, and we are permitted to take part in the victory and glory which arise out of Jesus' path of suffering.

It is in these places that our Lord Jesus is waiting for His bride. Our love for Him and our union with Him will increase if we do not fear to seek Him where He is to be found—in the places where He suffered. Then we shall really know the Bridegroom as He is, the Man of Sorrows. Then we shall experience His love and His solicitude. We shall feel Him sustaining and helping us to overcome the sins which bind us. Then we shall know the joy He gives even in the midst of suffering. He will be our complete abundance for everything we need.

But that happens only if we seek Him where He is to be found.

O Man of Sorrows, I adore
Your peerless grace and beauty:
All other splendours yield before
Your suff'ring's matchless glory.

O Man of Sorrows, I adore
How God Your pain transfigures,
As from Your face for evermore
Love's glory ever issues.

O Man of Sorrows, You have now
My heart for ever captured.
The beauty of Your suff'ring face
My whole heart has enraptured.

And I would love now only You,
Be one with You in suff'ring;
For if I love You, only You,
I'll share in Your self-off'ring.

O I would praise and honour You,
O Lamb, Your love confessing,
And always, always stay with You,
Your wounds for ever blessing.

How Should I Nourish
Bridal Love for Jesus?

I can only nourish the first love, bridal love, in so far as I
practise it. We know that the love of married couples can
easily diminish. It gets "rusty", if it is not expressed, if one
no longer uses words of love, if no longer one is lovingly
attentive, and if one no longer bestows love-gifts. Yes, love
begins to diminish, if we cease to think lovingly of the
other, if we no longer pronounce his name lovingly.

JESUS—THE MOST BEAUTIFUL NAME

The true bride of Jesus carries a secret in her heart. It is the
name of the Bridegroom. "Your name is oil poured out"
(Song of Solomon 1: 3). This I have known: When I let the
name of Jesus sound in my heart as the name of Him whom
I love above all else, when over and over again I pronounce
this name, my love for Him glows more and more. "Above
all names there is one Name. There is none equal to its fame
. . ." New songs continually flow from my heart. I have to
celebrate this name in song:

> *Praise and laud and honour pay*
> *To this holy Name of Jesus.*
> *All the heavens own its sway.*
> *Sing with us its splendid glory;*
> *Its all-conquering love adore,*
> *Jesus, Saviour, Christ our Lord!*

WJ 134

It was incomprehensible to me that we can claim this
name for ourselves, that we have a right to it. But if a bride
has difficulties, she can use her Bridegroom's name; this
name can open doors and remove all obstacles! The Bride-

groom rejoices when His bride claims His name. He rejoices when she is proud of having such a Bridegroom. My heart is overwhelmed whenever I call upon His name. What a Bridegroom I have! What a Prince of victory! He has fought the battle against Satan and has trampled him under foot. My Bridegroom is the risen Lord, who sits at the right hand of God. When we call upon His name, all bonds must burst asunder; the powers of Satan must flee.

Yes, "this is my beloved, and this is my friend," says the bride (Song of Solomon 5: 16b). He is the Almighty. He is the all-powerful Victor. When I call upon the name of Jesus, powers flee and afflictions give way. It is my privilege to call upon the name of His who is there to serve me in love. He lives completely for me, just as I live completely for Him. Jesus is here. He stretches forth His hand to me. He sets in action His almighty power for me. If I speak His name in my heart, something happens. Consider the effects of intercession on bound souls when simply the name "Jesus" or the words "Jesus is Victor" are repeated again and again! Prayers need not be long; indeed, in hours of greatest temptation and affliction we cannot make long prayers. Whenever I speak this name, peace comes into my heart. Then the answer comes; then the help comes in some way or other.

> *As often as I write the name of Jesus,*
> *a holy tremor passes through me*
> *with a joyous ardour of gratitude*
> *for the knowledge that Jesus is mine.*
> *Not until now did I really know*
> *what we have in Him.*

Johann Christoph Blumhardt (1805–1880)

Sometimes the name of Jesus sounds like a clarion in the heart of His bride. But at other times it is like the soft music of the lyre. There is so much ardour of love in this name; we possess it in our hearts as love's greatest gift. This name can never depart from us. It was such a precious thing for me to be able to say Jesus' name over and over again in my heart when I went through "desert periods" or when I was ill and it was hard to pray. No "wilderness state" could dim the glory of this name, because the bonds of love which join us to Him form a life eternal and divine which cannot be overcome.

What power lies in pronouncing the name of Jesus! It is the most effective prayer! Yet, we should not pronounce this name simply because it makes us happy, because it brings us peace and help. No, we should speak Jesus' name because we sense that it brings Him joy when we pronounce it lovingly. It draws us further into the bonds of love and strengthens them. A whisper of our love for Him (and is not our love always expressed in the naming of the beloved?), never remains unanswered. The One whom we love, and whose name we therefore speak so often lives and hears us, and if we lovingly utter His name, He answers and He offers His love to us. The love of the bride pleases Him and moves Him to return her love. He has said: 'He who loves me . . . I will love him . . . and we will come to him and make our home with him" (John 14; 21, 23). Jesus always answers songs which lovingly praise His name! How could it be otherwise? He cannot refuse to enter a heart that is waiting for Him in love. He must answer when we breathe His name!

It is of crucial importance that we practise our love for Jesus. We must not only speak His name silently or aloud, but also utter expressions of our love and gratitude for His love and for His sufferings. Yes, even at times when we do not feel equal to the task we should still adore Him. In so far as we sing and declare who He is, Jesus, our Bridegroom: the King of kings, the Lamb upon the highest throne, the mighty Prince of victory, the fairest of the sons of men, the Splendour of heaven, our hearts will be on fire with love for Him.

I have found that whenever I ceased to do this and no longer nourished the love of Jesus, the relationship of love to

Him became languid, and I ran the risk of lapsing from the first love, bridal love. There is great virtue in praising the nature of our Bridegroom. When we declare who He is, His glory shines upon us. If before we were lukewarm or depressed, now we are exalted and we begin to rejoice in Him again. Whenever we glorify Him, we can see that none can compare with Him. When we see the power of His love, His glory and His greatness, everything recedes which made His love seem weak and made Him seem to be a stranger.

To nourish bridal love means to practise the love of Jesus by uttering His name, by adoring Him, by declaring His glory. My love for Him is constantly being threatened, for here is one who begrudges us this greatest happiness—Satan. He prowls around like a roaring lion seeking a way to break into the chamber of the bride that he may destroy her fellowship of light and love with Jesus. He has many methods. He can rob us of our happiness by enticing us into temptation. He can bring men and the things of this world so alluringly close to us that we are drawn to them. But if we fall into his trap, we break the bond of love to Jesus, who does not tolerate a divided love. We are called to battle. By proclaiming who Jesus is, we set His glory over against these temptations and these alluring visions. Then the light of truth appears; we see who the true Love is. If we do not thus proclaim Him, we are lost, we lose the fellowship of life and love in Jesus; but he who nourishes bridal love and ever practises it in this way will reach his goal—the marriage supper of the Lamb.

Source of my joy, O Jesus most dear,
Jesus, Your name is the sweetest to hear,
Ringing with joy in my heart day and night.
Waking me up with the first rays of light.

Jesus, Your name is joyful to hear
And when we call on that name, You are here.
Take my heart, Lord, and Your home it shall be
Could any guest be more welcome to me?

True life now means to love only You,
And let my thoughts belong wholly to You.
You are the One I hold dearest and best,
And in Your love You allow me to rest.

Out of my heart comes sweet melody
So men Your likeness in my life will see
They too will choose You for their love alone
And this shall bring them to heaven's bright throne.

WJ 235

FOR YOU

Bridal love does not only mean lovingly uttering the name of Jesus; it also means doing everything out of love for Jesus. That makes the most difficult work easier. It turns the unpleasant into a source of joy. Our reactions are no longer determined simply by our natural talents and inclinations.

> *With Jesus the bitter becomes sweet.*
> *If the bitter has not yet become sweet for us,*
> *we are not in the fellowship of love with Jesus.*

The Lord wonderfully helped me to follow in this way, and He showed me how to do everything out of love for Him. When I was young I suffered severely from rheumatism, and at that time I was working as a travelling lecturer for the women's division of the German Student Christian Movement. Often I had to sleep on couches or made-up beds, and this gave me many sleepless nights. I could not fully accept this, and it seemed to spoil my fellowship with Jesus. Later on, I repented deeply that my love for Him was so small that I was not ready to bear a few inconveniences and discomforts for love of Him, and that I had been unwilling to trust in His love! I asked the Lord to give me an opportunity to atone for this, and to show Him what my love could bear, and so He led me into a travelling lectureship for a missionary society. During the second war I had to travel round Germany, including cities that were being subjected to heavy air-raids. Since I am by nature fearful, I found this a very difficult ministry. I had to travel, too, in crowded trains and stay in cold rooms.

But then the Lord gave me two little words which changed everything—an assertion of bridal love. It was a phrase which helped me greatly in all my troubles and even conquered my fear. The words were: "*For You!*" and they gave my life a new meaning. Whenever I realized that I was privileged to do and suffer all these things out of love "*For*

You"—the most difficult tasks seemed easy. Everything was transformed.

This happy state continued; the words "For You!" helped me to stay close to Jesus in my work all day long. They helped me to do all my tasks in His company. Whenever I began to be over-engrossed in my work and to do it apart from Him (even though that work was for God's Kingdom), those two words helped me. They were like wings transporting me to the One I loved. "For You—For You, my Lord Jesus!"

What power lies hidden in bridal love! It has immeasurable strength, because it unites us with the almighty Creator of the whole universe. Therefore, if we do everything for the love of Jesus (even peeling potatoes, or standing at the same machine day in and day out), and continually say "For You! For You!" then our work will have far-reaching effects—greater than we can imagine. The simplest work can bring forth fruit, if it is filled with everlasting power. It is only fellowship with Jesus that gives work this eternal value.

Why? Because love is the greatest power in the world. "Spiritual atomic power" lies in union with Jesus. Even if a man is ill, bed-ridden and seemingly inactive, he can accomplish great, far-reaching things and bring forth fruit for eternity if he will do and suffer everything in union with Jesus. It became my daily prayer as I began my day: "Let me do everything today together with You—working, speaking, thinking. Do not let me be separated from You today. Holy Spirit, admonish me when I cease to abide in Jesus." I know that our life can be fruitful only when we live in fellowship with Jesus.

Jesus, your Bridegroom, seeks fellowship with you. He entreats you:

Do everything for Me! Give Me your time!
Abide with Me all day long! Do not think, speak or do anything apart from me!
Understand that whenever we are separated it hurts Me. We are one!
Do not look at the work; look at Me!

Answer your Bridegroom:

Jesus, You are my everything!
I will talk with You and work for You!
I want to plan, consider and make all my decisions with You!
Nothing shall be done without You, lest You should become an Outcast.
Bind me tightly to You, so that nothing can separate us during the day: no work, no burden, no other interest, no joy.
May I evermore live in Your holy presence: For You are there!

COMMITTING OUR WILLS

Our bridal love will prosper only if we continually join ourselves to Jesus. The great union of love for Jesus lies in the dedication of the will. Bridal love proves its genuineness here: the soul must submit itself completely to the will of God, even when He frustrates its deepest wishes and desires, even when it does not understand what God is doing in its own life or in the lives of others. To nourish bridal love we must practise a continual dedication to His will.

I have often been led along paths which shattered all my hopes and desires. My prayers got no answer, and I could not understand what God was doing. But then I realized: the time has come when the reality of my love is to be tested. When I do not understand God, He is waiting for me to prove my love for Him by loving His will. I knew that the will of God is always good, for it springs from a heart of love. Therefore, His will *is* love. I began to sing of God's good will: "Your heart is goodness. Your will is only love. The paths that You have planned for me are good!" and this helped me to surrender my will completely to His. In spite of all my pain, peace came into my heart; the fellowship of love, the union with Jesus, was there again. I had raised a barrier against God as I rebelled or sighed, as I asked "why", and now that barrier had fallen.

We should always understand this: if our unity of will with God is broken, so is our unity of love with Jesus. We have ceased to "abide in Him". We have fallen out of the first love. Therefore, the nourishing of bridal love involves the avoidance of even the smallest rebellion against God's will. Bridal love is like a tender little plant. If the right soil is not there it will not grow—rather, it withers. And the right soil is the unity of the will with God. Do we realize how lovingly Jesus regards this little plant in our hearts? Often He regards us so sadly from far off, because we have not kept close to Him, and we have broken the unity of will.

Should we not strive every day for this dedication of our will? In no other way have we such a wonderful opportunity to bring joy to our Bridegroom.

Every time we dedicate our will to God,
in the events of life,
the union of love takes place.
This is an absolute and certain union,
and therefore the purest and the highest.

Jesus, Master, I would love Thee,
Thou my glory, treasure be!
Take my will, let it obey Thee,
For I am Thy property.

Let me only live to love Thee,
Love Thee only, Thee alone;
My free will I now do give Thee,
All I am to be Thine own.

Jesus, Lord, to give Thee pleasure
Is my life's one single aim;
Nothing else will I now treasure
But to glorify Thy Name.

With Thy life my life is quickened,
I would only live for Thee.
I have now my will surrendered,
Out of love I gave it Thee.

WHERE I WILL DWELL . . .

What a wonderful promise! God the Lord, who calls Himself the Husband of His chosen people, proclaims: "The Lord has chosen Zion; he has desired it for his habitation: 'This is my resting place for ever; here I will dwell, for I have desired it' " (Psalm 132: 13, 14). And Jesus makes the same promise when He tells His bride, the soul that loves Him: "If a man loves Me . . . My Father will love him, and We will come to him and make Our home with him" (John 14: 23).

The Lord is seeking a place, a heart, where He may abide, where He can make His dwelling-place. That verse from Psalm 132 hung for a long time on the walls of the room where our Girls' Bible Studies had their meetings during the revival in 1944–45. At that time, I wanted to have this verse before my eyes, because it expressed the highest desire and the most fervent longing of my heart. My deepest longing was that the Lord would say to me also: "Here I will dwell, for I have desired it." It seemed to me that the Lord could never say a more wonderful thing to any soul than that He desired to live there, because it pleased Him.

In John 14, Jesus tells us where He wants to dwell; it is in the soul that loves Him. It is love that draws Him to take up His abode in such a heart. What a wonderful prospect! It is love that keeps Him there. This love does not consist of feelings, but of the unity of will with Him. This means that our hearts must be constantly inclined to Him. It is a love which is dedicated to Him even along difficult paths. Therefore, it is a love which is united with Him.

> *"I come to live within you,"*
> *God's Son, the Lord Christ Jesus*
> *Says this to ev'ry Christian soul.*
> *"Prepare for Me a lodging,*
> *With ardent love and longing,*
> *That I may with your soul unite."*

"Make ready your heart's chamber,
Put far all earthly clamour,
Silence all worldly longings now.
Upon you take My quietness
Eternity's own stillness,
And My approaching footsteps hear."

WJ 226

Yet, we may lose Him who inclines Himself to us. The Lord can also "pull up stakes" and depart from us, if our love for Him grows cold. He will only live in hearts that love Him. There alone does He desire to dwell.

To love Him means to give Him first place. It means that He is our greatest good. Our hearts are inclined towards Him. But we must watch and be alert, lest the cares and joys of this world overwhelm us. When such things begin to take first place in our hearts, our Lord Jesus departs, and our heart is now filled with other things. To speak in a figure, the innermost chamber of our heart is His dwelling-place, and none of the things which interest us and excite us can be allowed to penetrate into that sanctuary where He lives and reigns. It must remain inviolate from all that would disturb us. It must remain in peace, because He who lives there is Peace.

Every true bride of Jesus makes the innermost chamber of her heart a shrine. Her greatest joy is that He has promised to make His dwelling in the hearts of those who love Him. For those who have bridal love there is no greater fear than the loss of this first love through being caught up in the world's cares and joys. If they lose their first love, He can no longer dwell in their hearts. They tremble lest this happen to them. They tremble lest they lose His indwelling. They tremble lest work and pleasure, suffering—even for others—and joys engross them utterly.

The bride of Jesus longs that nothing should drive her Bridegroom from her heart. She knows that He is a jealous Lord, and that He will be the only Ruler of our heart. He will not have us ruled by the troubles, cares, people and things of this world. That is why the bridal soul fights "to the point of shedding blood" (Heb. 12: 4) so that nothing else may enthral her and so that He may maintain His right to rule and dwell in her heart. Her greatest joy and happiness is that He lives in her and gives her the deepest peace, no matter what her troubles may be, no matter what demands are made upon her. She ever longs to be more and more joined to Him, He in her and she in Him. She lives all her life with Him.

The greatest gift, the greatest pledge, of the Bridegroom Jesus: His indwelling! That is sufficient for us. He lives in the deepest region of the heart; He is there even in the darkest night, when we can feel nothing and He seems to be far away. He is there. What a wonderful consolation! Is there anything greater? Even when we know "the dark night of the soul" or suffer periods of dryness, we may have this certainty: He who is Life lives in me. In the night life is born.

It is especially in times of darkness, when temptations and hardships threaten to overcome us, that Jesus, our Bridegroom beholds us in love and watches intently to see how we stand our ground and endure. Shall we prove ourselves truly to be His bride? Shall we hold fast to His indwelling? His love demands that in these trials we really prove ourselves His bride; that is, that we should not be wrapped up in ourselves, nor let our feelings and thoughts and temptations get the better of us, but rather that we should rely upon His presence, His indwelling, which is more powerful than all temptations and hardships and burdens. Thus our times of darkness will only serve to join us more closely to Him.

Even in the darkest times we may be certain that Jesus is there, even if we do not actually feel His presence. If we offer all our cares to Him, if we submit ourselves to Him who lives within us, He will live in us. It is in the driest times, in the times of greatest hardship, that we may bring Him the choicest fruit.

If we do not wish to die,
Our love for Jesus will die.
If we choose death,
The divine life of love will blossom—
because Jesus will find room in us.

FOR TIMES OF DARKNESS

Jesus, the Bridegroom, encourages the soul that loves
Him:

Endure!
Keep fighting!
Look towards the goal—you will get your reward!
Am I not enough for you?
Will you not suffer with Me?
Look at Me, and your trials will be bearable!
I am really here! Oh, believe Me!

The bride of Jesus answers:
Yes, You are here. That is enough for me. Amen.

TO EXPERIENCE HIS PRESENCE

O, my Lord Jesus, Thy presence
Bringeth great peace to our hearts.
Thy gracious appearance maketh us so blessed
That body and soul become
Joyous and thankful.

Christian Gregor (1723–1801).

Those who have bridal love for Jesus know the blessed hours when Jesus draws near to us. Our love yearns for these times, because love is never satisfied, can never have enough. We long to have our Beloved close to us, and truly there are times when the love of Jesus visits us. Many have witnessed this. Those whose bridal love for Jesus is deep have known the closeness of His love in special ways.

Satan and his evil spirits can pervade material things; they can fill rooms and enter men. One can sometimes clearly sense their presence or even hear them. How much more will Jesus draw close to those who love Him! He will dwell in their hearts. He also can pervade places, so that one senses that His Spirit is resting there. But He can also come to us sometimes in such a way that not only do we feel His presence, but our whole being is imbued with His love.

God is eternal, holy and unapproachable; but the Holy Scriptures declare that He is also Love, and that it is this that moves Him to reveal Himself to us poor human beings. The miracle of God's revelation began with the history of Israel. Moses was permitted to experience that God spoke to Him "face to face, as a man speaks to his friend" (Exod. 33: 11). His face shone because of this encounter with the holy God (Exod. 34: 29). Over and over again God showed Himself. He worked in men. He drew so close to them in His holiness that Isaiah thought that he would die in the holy presence of God (Isa. 6: 5), and of the disciple John it is written that he fell down as though dead, when he saw Jesus (Rev. 1: 17). To this day a meeting with God can be as real as this, when He comes to us as the Bridegroom.

Most blessed and most holy encounter with the Godhead! It can transform a man. God imprints His seal upon a human being. This is the most wonderful thing that can happen to him. Blessed are they whom God has so touched with His love that they fell prostrate before Him as sinners. Blessed are those whom God has so touched with His love that their hearts have burned within them.

We have heard the words of some great lovers of Jesus. Francis of Assisi, for example, knew the blessedness of this encounter. The sweetness of Jesus flowed through his spirit, soul and body and gave him such delight that his face began to shine and he concealed it under his hood. Even if such cases are exceptional, Jesus, the Lover, approaches each bridal soul in His own special way.

Before Your feet, O Lord, I lie adoring,
To greet You, Lord, my soul to heav'n is soaring;
You are so fair, so full of tenderness,
My heart is set on fire by all Your loveliness.

To none on earth nor cherubim in heaven
Is knowledge of Your beauty fully given.
Beside it other glories all grow dim,
How blessed am I, for I am greatly loved by Him!

So here I taste the life of highest heaven,
For with You, Lord, such joy and bliss is given.
The earth its great Creator's glory sings;
But in Your heart Your bride sees yet more wondrous things.

O Jesus, focus of the earthly story,
Resplendent mirror of God's pow'r and glory,
Before You, Lord, in worship now I fall;
For me the vision of Your face is all in all.

WJ 233

THE "DARK" LOVE

The blissful experiences of Jesus' presence are a foretaste of heaven, which we could not bear for long here on earth. Therefore, the Bridegroom will at times withdraw from the bridal soul, although He always dwells within her. He withdraws His perceptible presence and leads her along dark paths, as it is written in the Song of Solomon: the bride is "coming up from the wilderness" (8: 5). She is "leaning upon her beloved". Her soul is parched. She sought Him and did not find Him. It became dark in her soul. He stayed far from her. But in this the Bridegroom proves that He really loves His bride with a true bridal love; by this means He makes her more lovely and more lovable than she was before. For on this desert path, her Bridegroom far away, she knows her poverty and weakness. She is humiliated. She becomes humble. She acknowledges her frailties and her sins, and weeps over them anew. Her tears are more precious to the Lord than anything else. Mary Magdalene washed Jesus' feet with her tears and Jesus gave His judgment: she "loved much". She was the great sinner and the great lover.

Yes, Jesus seeks love; He thirsts for love. He knows that bridal love must be touched by His love. But He wants it to grow; He wants it to be purer and stronger. So He withdraws from us from time to time. He allows our emotional longings, which seek for the bliss of His love, to wither and die. If the bride can still tread her path faithfully when she cannot satisfy her desire to "feel", then her love for Jesus will be proved. And when she "comes up from the wilderness", her Bridegroom will receive her anew. He will overwhelm her and bless her with His presence.

Deep mysteries and infinite treasures lie buried in the depths of bridal love. Whoever would discover these treasures must dare to plunge into the depths of the sea. It is the way of "the night of suffering". It is the way of the cross, of the fellowship of sufferings, which reveals these treasures to us. If Jesus said to the disciples who wanted to share His glory on the throne: "Are you able to drink the cup that I am to drink?" (Matt. 20: 22), He also says this to those who want to know the reality of His grace, to taste His love, and experience the most intimate unity of love with Him: "Are you ready to drink the cup of suffering?" Suffering brings glory—but not only above. Whoever will go the way of the cross with Jesus will begin to taste glory here.

Grant that I may show how blessed it is to love Thee,
to suffer with Thee, to weep with Thee,
to be united with Thee forever in praise.

Calvin (1509–1564)

THE FELLOWSHIP OF HIS SUFFERINGS

Nourishing bridal love for Jesus means above all to meditate upon His sufferings. Jesus, the Bridegroom, is the Man of Sorrows, and this He will always be. Above He still bears His wounds; in the heavens He still appears as the Lamb that was slain (Rev. 5: 6). Today, because He is the same yesterday and today, He still suffers, because we sons of men grieve Him. I can only love Jesus if I have really taken His sufferings into my heart, if I am grieved by His past and present sufferings, which my sin and the sin of the world bring upon Him.

Before I entered bridal love for Jesus, I knew about His sufferings, and often I was moved by them. But they had not become a vital part of my heart. When I learned to love Jesus, I understood the burdens of His heart. Today it is still filled with sorrow over His people—believers and unbelievers alike. Jesus is still suffering, because so many grieve Him by their wanton sinning, because so many of His own dispute and quarrel and defame His name. He suffers through those who declare Him dead—yes, even today in the Church. He suffers through the millions who hate Him and treat Him with scorn and pierce His heart with arrows of hate. He suffers through those who once were close to Him and loved Him, but who then forsook their first love and preferred other things to Him.

Love seeks to console and comfort the Beloved when He suffers. This is love's most precious act. It cannot bear to see the One it loves, honours and worships so often dishonoured, reviled and insulted. That is why it was not until I learned to love Jesus that my heart was set on fire to do something for Him, to use all my power so that people might be brought to love Him and give Him the glory. My grief about Jesus' sufferings moved me to write about them so that others might understand how He suffers, and might offer Him their love to comfort Him.

God receives so little gratitude and adoration for the beauty of His creation. This led me to build small chapels to His glory in popular beauty spots, in spite of many obstacles. The desire to make the sufferings of Jesus more realistic to people today led me to establish a "Garden of Jesus' Sufferings" on our Land of Canaan* where the Stations of the Cross are depicted. Many come here to meditate on His sufferings, while others learn for the first time of His sorrows, and all of them will be inspired in different ways to work for Jesus in gratitude for His sufferings. We can never have bridal love for Jesus without having also a living relationship to His sufferings. Jesus is the Man of Sorrows, the Man of wounds. He who really loves, lives in His sufferings. He grieves over and laments over these sufferings. He thanks Jesus for them. Like a true bride, who does nothing apart from her bridegroom, he enters into the fellowship of His sufferings.

> *I love Thee, O my Saviour, Lamb of God,*
> *Who wounded sore, the path of suff'ring trod,*
> *By evil men blasphemed and put to scorn,*
> *They mock Thee, holy Lord, with crown of thorn,*
> *Beloved Lord, how I love Thee!*
>
> *I love Thee Lord, no longer will I stray,*
> *But at Thy side stand true to Thee alway,*
> *To suffer for Thy sake my soul prepare,*
> *In gratitude for all that Thou didst bear,*
> *O hear my prayer, Lord, hear my prayer.*

What is the fellowship of His sufferings? Let us look at the life of the Apostle Paul. When he claimed to be a true servant of Jesus, he listed all the sufferings which he had borne on the way with Jesus: poverty, fears, hunger,

* "Canaan", named after the Biblical land of Canaan, is the land of the Evangelical Sisterhood of Mary located in the suburbs of Darmstadt, Western Germany. With its twenty-two acres is a centre serving to glorify the name of God. (See Basilea Schlink, *Realities*—Lakeland 1967).

disappointments, deprivations, disgrace (2 Cor. 11: 23ff). As I began to tread the path with Jesus my Bridegroom, it seemed to me as though He were standing there as the Lonely and Forsaken One asking: Will you go with Me and share My life of suffering? My poverty, deprivation, disgrace, lowliness? Entering the fellowship of His sufferings is the fruit of love. Love willingly treads the path of the Bridegroom even if it is a path of thorns. Here love for Jesus is seen in action. If we go this way, we nourish bridal love and become more and more closely joined to Jesus. So I found, after I told Jesus that I would go the way of the cross with Him.

The Lord really did let me taste some of His sufferings along His way. I bore disdain, slander, hate and disgrace for His name's sake. He let me taste the sufferings of poverty, which humiliate us, diminish our influence and make us dependent upon others. Having chosen His way, we Sisters of Mary had no money and therefore no influence and no ability to get the things we needed for the Sisterhood and its work. He let me discover what it is like to go without sleep and without food for His sake; but He let me discover too that the fellowship of His sufferings brings us into the fellowship of His love. I cannot describe how close Jesus came to me on this path, or the generous way in which He gave me His love. Not in vain is it called the "*fellowship* of His sufferings". As we suffer with Jesus, we are brought into a close fellowship, a union of love, with Him.

Jesus stands in the sight of everyone who would like to love Him and become a bridal soul. He stands as the Man of Sorrows who still today treads His path of sorrows over the earth, derided, humiliated, abased, forsaken. He asks: Who will go with Me?—I am so alone. Who will be My bride and My companion? Who will share My sufferings with Me —humiliation, disgrace, lowliness and poverty?

This is how we start on the way of the fellowship of His sufferings. For many in our time it will end in martyrdom. In times of persecution it is plainest to see that the fellowship of His sufferings is the fellowship of His love. Men and women aflame with love, a love which showed itself mighty in word and deed in the midst of persecution and suffering, proved that only one power is greater than the power of the most terrible suffering, the power of love for Jesus. They have shown the truth of this verse from the Song of Solomon: "Love is strong as death" (8: 6). Love is stronger than anything else, because it is immortal. In a royal and victorious way, it overcomes all sufferings, all crosses and all tortures. It brings triumphant joy.

Today we approach the time of martyrdom. Almost two-thirds of humanity is already under the influence or regime of communistic atheism. Men are hated and persecuted for the confession of Jesus Christ, and even in the so-called Christian countries the spirit of Antichrist is on the march, and not only ridicules God and Jesus Christ, but also seeks to use violence against believers and to exterminate everything Christian. Soon the atheistic, antichristian wave will roll over all countries, just as Jesus prophesied for the last times, the times in which we are now living: "You will be hated by all nations for my name's sake" (Matt. 24: 9). That is why there is nothing so important in our time as the love for Jesus, bridal love, which has known something of the fellowship of His sufferings. Otherwise we are lost. Otherwise we have no strength to endure suffering for His sake.

Many cases could be mentioned of believers who had not entered into the fellowship of His sufferings. In the hour of trial they either denied Him or forsook Him. They were the folk who earlier on had not been willing to suffer or sacrifice for Jesus' sake; they did not want to sacrifice their position or income, their honour, livelihood or family. Such people, who had no opportunity to escape martyrdom, broke down completely in despair. They had nothing of the joy of the first Christians.

Not for nothing is it written that those who love Him will receive the crown of life. Those who love Jesus are conquerors even in the deepest suffering and martyrdom. If,

83

therefore, one should sell all his possessions to attain this love (Song of Solomon 8: 7), he would still have given too little, for it is such a precious treasure. It is worth everything Because Jesus knows the treasure He is offering, He can justly call us to take up our cross and follow Him in the fellowship of His sufferings. He knows that He is offering eternal life. He knows that He will repay us a hundredfold for everything we forsake out of love when we follow Him on the way of the cross. He will repay us while we are on earth and even more in eternal glory.

With You the Cross's way I'll go,
With You I'll share its pain and woe,
With You go into darkness.
With You I will one day arise,
Be throned with You in paradise,
With You I am united.

With You I'll suffer pain and death,
With You will draw my last slow breath,
Living with You, and dying.
With You I'll know the joy of love,
With You I'll soar to heav'n above
And taste life everlasting.

With You I'll live from hour to hour
And find Your love has healing pow'r
Whene'er my heart is wounded.
With You I'll love the long dark night
For it will bring me heaven's light,
With You light conquers darkness.

With You I'll bear the sense of loss,
With You I'll suffer any cross,
So I Your heart may enter.
With You I will accept all this,
For it will bring me glorious bliss,
The love of God eternal.

84

The Mirror of Conscience
For Bridal Love for Jesus

WHEN DO YOU HAVE THE FIRST LOVE,
REAL BRIDAL LOVE FOR JESUS?

When you lovingly pronounce in your heart—consciously and unconsciously—the one name: "Jesus" and when you are moved to give Him new names of love: "My Dearest, my Crowning Glory, my King, my Life, my Joy, my One and my All."

When your heart is continually astonished and amazed, knowing who your Bridegroom is, when you are compelled to worship Him.

When your heart rejoices and shouts with joy again and again, "I am chosen, chosen to be the bride of Jesus."

When you kneel at the foot of His cross mourning ever anew over your sins, filled with gratitude and love, unable to realize that you have been forgiven, unable to realize what He has done for you through His suffering.

When you desire only to be loved by Him.

When He alone captivates you. When only His presence can bring joy into your heart.

When you no longer desire to spend your leisure with others or to use it for your favourite pastimes or hobbies, but desire to be with Him.

When you feel drawn to suffer or to sacrifice for Him. When you seek new ways to bring your gifts to Him.

When, facing the choice between Him and the people and things you love, you choose Him without further reflection.

When you do everything in your daily round together with Him.

When you undertake difficult tasks gladly and lovingly with the two little words: "For You—for You!"

When Jesus really is the joy of your heart, and this joy shines in your face and in your whole being.

When nothing can make you so happy as when Jesus receives glory and love from men and the way is paved for His kingdom.

When you no longer seek to please men, but Him only.

When you no longer do anything for your own self-satisfaction, pleasure and honour, but rather live only to give Him the glory and joy.

When you completely dedicate your will and your wishes to Him.

When you constantly devise new ways of making Jesus happy by offering Him sacrifices, showing your love and adoration in prayer and song, spending yourself for His ministry and serving others in love for His name's sake.

When your heart is filled to the brim with longing for the day of His appearing when you will see Him face to face.

When you love no one, nor anything but Jesus. For Jesus accepts only your undivided love.

When you trust Him, as a bride trusts her bridegroom: He lives for me. He protects me. He stands up for me. He does everything for me. He cares for me and all that concerns me.

When your fellowship with Jesus is closer than any other.

When Jesus has become the most intimate Friend of your heart and life.

When you can say, in losing everything that makes your life worth living: "So long as I have You—I have all I need."

When you zealously fight against your sins through love for Him, to bring Him joy by becoming a beautiful bride.

When your heart weeps over your sin, because you have hurt and disappointed Him.

When you follow Him without question upon His path, as a true bride would follow her bridegroom.

When lovingly and joyfully you tread His way of sorrow and take upon yourself His way of poverty, lowliness, humiliation, obedience, dependence and purity, because to suffer these is a sign that you belong to Him.

When your heart cannot bear to see Him suffer and you want to suffer with Him, console Him, and do the things that bring Him joy.

When His wounds are precious to you and you adore them, as a sign of His glory and His love, a revelation of His true nature, spending itself in suffering.

When you are always waiting: waiting to receive Him in everyday life, waiting for His presence, waiting for His coming again to His whole bridal host, waiting for the day of the marriage supper of the Lamb.

*   *   *

God, the only Spouse of my soul—
God, who makes my soul fruitful for eternal life,
Him alone will I love and nothing other than Him.
Augustine (354–430)

WHEN DOES BRIDAL LOVE FOR JESUS GROW DIM? WHEN DO I LEAVE MY FIRST LOVE?

When I let cares enter my heart and lodge there, they smother the flame of bridal love.

When I let accusations against my neighbour lodge in my heart and nourish them, they choke bridal love.

When I seek my own satisfaction and honour in my works and deeds, bridal love disappears from my heart.

When I am not ready to commit my will to Him, He withdraws from me and my love grows dim.

When I do not confess my sin and am not willing to humble myself, I lose His grace; my love no longer receives nourishment from Him; it fades away.

When I rebel against chastisements and sufferings, the relationship of love to Jesus is disrupted. I have fallen from the first love.

When some earthly thing, a person or an object, becomes my idol, when my thoughts and my love keep circling around it, I have fallen from the first love.

When I devote my best time, put forth my best efforts, and devote my interests and my talents more to something else other than to Jesus, my bridal love will die.

When something entirely captures my attention and takes up all my time and energy, Jesus stands outside. The bridal relationship is disrupted; I have fallen from the first love.

When I no longer live according to God's commandments, I show that I do not love the One who gave them. Bridal love is disrupted.

When I can no longer weep for my sins, I do not belong to my Bridegroom, who is the Saviour of sinners. The unity of love is broken; the flame of love is ready to die.

When I no longer hate my sin and no longer fight against it, I do not love Him who died for our sins. The bridal relationship is disrupted.

When there is jealousy, envy, hatred, bitterness, impurity, falsehood or egoism in my life, I am shut out from the Kingdom of God and shut off from Jesus. My bridal love will wither up like a flower.

When I live more in earthly things, in everyday life, in my work, in my cares and joys than in heavenly things, I withdraw from my Bridegroom, Jesus, who is the King of heaven. Bridal love dies.

When I doubt Jesus' love, help and power, the union with Him is disrupted and bridal love grows dim.

When the crosses and the sacrifices which are demanded of me become irksome, my love is ready to die: for love drives us to sacrifice.

When I have become spiritually satiated, when I am no longer hungry to hear about Jesus and to worship Him, as a true bride would hunger to hear about her bridegroom, I am no longer a bride.

When I am no longer dismayed and grieved that the body of my Bridegroom is rent asunder, that His honour has been trodden under foot, that His name is blasphemed, that He is not loved, then I show that I am not the bride of Jesus. My bridal love is gone.

Nevertheless I have somewhat against thee,
Because thou hast left thy First Love.
Remember therefore from whence thou art fallen,
*   and repent,*
And do the first works.

Rev. 2: 4, 5 (AV)

How Can I Bring Joy to My Bridegroom Jesus and Comfort Him?

To make Jesus happy and comfort Him—is such a thing possible? Yes; just as we can grieve God's heart (Gen. 6:6), so we can also bring Him joy and comfort Him, especially when He is grieved. Out of the Psalm of sorrows, we hear the voice of Jesus speaking to us: "I looked for comforters, but I found none" (Psalm 69: 20). How can we become comforters? Perhaps we are looking for great deeds and sacrifices which we may offer to bring Him joy and comfort. But there are many other things we can do, and opportunities we can take.

I can bring joy to my Bridegroom Jesus and comfort Him:

When I can speak these words in suffering: "I want to suffer out of gratitude and love for You!"

When in my fears I can say: "I trust You. You have conquered my fear."

When in my spiritual death I can say: "You are my life!"

When in the face of my bondage to sin I can say: "You are my Redeemer. I believe in Your victory!"

When I am prepared to lie at the foot of the cross as a sinner condemned by God and man.

When I do not despair in the midst of failure but continue to sing of His sacrifice which can make me free.

When in great affliction I can say: "My affliction is not greater than You, my Helper."

When I can say along the bitter path: "I know that You will make the bitter sweet."

When I say in great temptation: "I will cling to You and go the way with You to the end. I believe in Your love."

When I can say in spiritual darkness or at times when I feel forsaken by God: "Nothing can separate me from You—I am a part of You."

When I declare on paths of chastisement: 'I thank You, my Bridegroom. It is Your love which seeks to bless me on this path and prepare me for glory."

When I am overworked, spending all my energy in tasks and can still say: "I will not let You go from my thoughts!"

When I have much to do, even too much, and yet nevertheless can say: "Thank you Lord."

When I have much to bear and can say: "Give me more! I will gladly bear anything with You, for You!"

When I love my cross.

When I celebrate His victory in the midst of my own defeat.

When I am concerned with His suffering, and not my own.

When I in my times of prayer become absorbed in His sufferings and meditate upon them lovingly.

When I am concerned above all to hear what He has to say to me.

When I do something for another out of love for Him.

When I do not complain about anything, but rather thank Him because He has my best interests at heart.

When I think about His concerns more than about my own.

When I speak words of love to Him, even when I am not in the spirit of devotion.

When I make every effort to save souls for Him and to set them afire with love for Him.

When I spend myself, sacrificing time, money, strength and honour to spread the glory of His name.

When I do not forget the good things He has done for me and continually count my blessings with gratitude.

When I accept His wishes, His will and His commandments as holy and obligatory for me and surrender my own will and desires to Him ever anew.

When I do not seek to please, to be loved and esteemed by men, but rather only seek to please Him.

When I have no desires except what He desires, what He gives or what He withholds.

When I bear testimony to Him, His love, His sufferings.

When I bring Him my adoration in word or song.

When I bring Him a sacrifice of love.

When there is darkness in me and around me and I can say: "You are my Light, which will not be put out—that is sufficient for me."

When I am in a place where there is no way out and can declare: "You are the Way. You have made a way. I trust You."

When I forgive those who have hurt me or wronged me, as He has forgiven me.

When I bear difficult people in patience and love, as He always bears me.

When I do good things for others who make life difficult for me, just as He does good things for me.

When I gladly do things that are hard, because I love Him.

When I continually think about Him and give Him my love.

When I am humiliated, disdained and abased and can still bless Him that I may tread His path.

When I prefer Him to all else, because He is my only Joy.

When neither cares nor afflictions can drive Him out of my heart.

When I humble myself before God and man.

When I believe in His love in every situation.

As the Bridegroom rejoices over the Bride,
So shall your God rejoice over you.

Isa. 62: 5

Bridal Love – A Consuming Fire

The love of the bridal soul for Jesus is like a burning fire. It glows with great power. It is like "a most vehement flame" (Song of Solomon 8: 6). Why? Because the bride loves the fairest of all, the One most worthy of love. She must spend her whole life for Him. His wishes enthral her so much that she must do everything to fulfil them. His desire is to free those who are bound, to bring men home to their Father. His longing is that His kingdom may spread the world over. He wants the flame of spiritual power to blaze everywhere so that God's kingdom may be seen on earth.

Because Jesus' love encompasses the whole world, His bride has been entrusted with an immense, world-wide commission. The zeal for these things for which He gave His life burns in His heart, and He would kindle such a flame in every true bride. He wants her gladly to give her life too, so that souls may be saved and the way prepared for the Kingdom of God.

> Bridal love for Jesus
> is always in motion,
> an ever-increasing ardour:
> An ever-increasing desire
> to bestow gifts upon the Beloved,
> an ever-increasing desire
> to spend oneself for the Beloved.
> Love is the opposite
> of satiety and contentedness.

Those who love in a bridal fashion, then, are they who press on ardently so that God's Kingdom might appear. They are never satisfied with the *status quo*. They always have new aims and hopes for their faith, because everything they have so far done for their Bridegroom seems to them to be insufficient. They must work zealously that He may be more loved and honoured. Thus they shatter the complacency of sleeping Christians. They arouse them; they wrench them from their selfish striving for their own sanctification, so that they may begin to put in the central place the One who loves them, and devote their lives to His concerns and His honour.

Burning with bridal love, they are always alert and ready to spend their time and energy to carry their Bridegroom's fire into new places. They see every opportunity; in faith they continually set their feet upon new territory. They serve the King of kings, whose domain is the whole universe. Therefore, "the world is their parish" and their hearts are large enough to serve the whole world's needs and sufferings. The bride of Jesus has tasted the Kingdom of Heaven in fellowship with her Bridegroom. She knows that He came to establish that kingdom on earth. She cannot rest until God's kingdom dawns everywhere in the midst of this world's darkness. She is content only when she can see the Kingdom of Heaven rising resplendently in every possible place. She uses every hour and wastes no time. She treads paths of repentance, of deepest humiliation and affliction, if only the way for God's Kingdom may be prepared. She knows that she can only bring the kingdom of God to others if she ceases to bar the way with a sense of her own importance.

The bride of Jesus radiates the brightness of the Kingdom of Heaven wherever she goes. She is set on fire with the love of the Bridegroom and enkindles hearts everywhere. No one is a bride of Jesus who is not like a flame glowing with zeal for the Kingdom of God.

Yet she does not glow in and of herself, for like everyone else she is a poor, erring sinner. But she lives in union with Him who is flaming Love and who has become her Bridegroom. She becomes the grain of wheat that dies so that it may bear fruit. Together with her Bridegroom she builds the Kingdom of Heaven, the kingdom of life, of radiance and joy. Having been called to His side, she is taken up into His life. She let herself be called away from everything else, that she might go through life at the side of Him who has become her All, and so she does not have to rely upon herself. She need not calculate her talents, abilities and personality. She does not need to consider what is available and what is possible. She has only to reckon with Him, with the power of His love. Jesus, the Source of life for all men, is the Fire of God, the Sun of the whole world, the Hearth of love. Will He not inflame the heart of His bride as well?

The Bridegroom says:

I came to cast fire upon the earth;
And would that it were already kindled!

Luke 12: 49

O that Thy fire would soon be kindled,
Thou inexpressible Lover,
and soon the whole world should know,
that Thou art King, Lord and God.

George Friedrich Fickert (1758–1815)

When is Bridal Love for Jesus Set Aflame?

Your bridal love will be the sooner set aflame the more you behold the Bridegroom Jesus, the more you meditate on Him, the more your heart converses with Him, and your tongue declares who He is.

Spend much of your time picturing Jesus. Meditate especially on Him as the Man of Sorrows. His suffering reveals all His beauty. Proclaim, declare, ever anew witness who your Bridegroom Jesus is, and your heart will be even more and more inspired to love Him. You will understand who He is, comprehend His love and His beauty and return His love.

Your bridal love will be deepened at every fresh encounter with your Bridegroom, as you converse with Him and share with Him. Seek frequent encounters with Jesus. The more you use every possible free moment for prayer, and meet Him and speak to Him, to pour out your heart to Him, and to listen inwardly to what He has to say to you, the more your love will grow. Your bridal love will be deepened as you make more room for Jesus. Tear vain things from your heart, the things your heart esteems. Make room for Him so that He can live there and display His love. Over and over again it is a matter of putting behind you things which are dear to you, so that you may retain the dearest, your Bridegroom.

Your bridal love will be set aflame through dedication. Whenever you dedicate something to Jesus, the bond of love for Him will become more intimate. In the dedication of your will and your desires there is sacrifice, and the more you sacrifice for Jesus, the more closely you are joined to Him. Your love will burn brightly as you join your will anew to His, for love grows stronger in unity. The flame of love blazes more fiercely as you sacrifice your will upon the altar.

Your bridal love will be set aflame when you stay close by your Bridegroom, that is, when you share His way with Him. His way consists of certain "stepping stones": poverty, humiliation, love of the cross, humility, obedience, purity. When you set your feet upon one of these "stepping stones" which He once stepped on, you will be more closely united with Him, for you are treading His path with Him. But whenever you set your foot upon some "stepping stone" which is not one of His, you will be separated from Him. All your adoration of the Bridegroom and your talk about bridal love will be of no avail. In that moment the flame of love dies out.

Your bridal love will be deepened when you put your trust in Jesus your Bridegroom. Trust honours Him, and brings Him down to you in great love. Then His loving inclination to you will set your love aflame. You can offer Him your trust above all when it is dark in your heart, when He no longer answers, when you feel that He is far away and no longer concerned about you. You can offer Him your trust in His love when you no longer understand His ways, because your hopes have been disappointed and everything seems meaningless. If then you can still put your trust in Him and say: "You are with me; You are in my heart; we are united for ever; nothing can separate us" then this steadfastness in love will make your flame of love glow brightly. Your bridal love will have stood the test.

Your bridal love will be set aflame when you do everything together with Jesus all day long. Do the smallest and most ordinary things with Him. Do the seemingly senseless things with Him. Everything you do with Him will inspire a new and precious love for Him, a constant love which will be evident in everyday life. So all day long do everything with Him.

Your bridal love will be deepened if you do everything with the words: *"For You!"* Thus you will devote your love to His difficult tasks. If these two little words spring from your heart, especially when the task or the way seems difficult, they will fan the flame of love like a bellows.

Your bridal love will be set aflame when you lie at the feet of the Crucified One, the Man of Sorrows, in repentance. A lack of repentance quenches the flame of love; repentance fans it. Repentance is fuel for love's fire; makes it burn brightly. Repentance opens our eyes so that we can see Jesus as the Man of Sorrows, bearing His wounds for the sake of our sins. Repentance brings us to see His beauty in suffering. It sets our love for Him on fire again. Only eyes which weep for sin have been opened and can really see Jesus in His beauty. If your eyes are dry, you may be able to speak much about Him, but you will not see Him with your heart and really love Him.

Your bridal love will be set aflame when repentance turns you about and leads you back to Jesus. Repentance will lead you to do something that will bring Him joy, something which is the opposite of the sin which caused Him so much grief. His joy over your deed will fill your heart and increase your love for Him. Every act of repentance adds fuel to the fire of love.*

Your bridal love will be set aflame when you as bride reflect upon the most important thing about your Bridegroom—His love, which suffered in the days of His flesh and suffers now, until all are loved home. Meditate, therefore, upon Jesus' Passion then and now. Consider how much He had to suffer while He was on earth; consider how much He suffers today. Read about His Passion; bring it into your prayer life, and your love will increase, become intimate, tender. Your love will sympathize with the sufferings of Jesus, and enter into them. It will inspire you to comfort Him; it will constrain you to suffer for Him so that you may console and comfort Him in His sufferings.†

Your bridal love will be deepened when you are filled with the thought of the coming of Jesus, when you live for

* Basilea Schlink, *Repentance—the Joy-filled Life* (Lakeland, 1967).
† Basilea Schlink, *In Our Midst* (Evangelical Sisterhood of Mary, 1970.

His second coming. When the coming of the Bridegroom is imminent, the heart of the bride leaps for joy—that is certain. When you are no longer expectant of His coming, the flame of your love will grow dim. Expect Him! Watch for Him daily—for daily He draws near. But also wait for Him to come and take you home when your life draws towards its end. Then He will embrace you, and you will see Him face to face. Await Him as the King and Bridegroom, who will come again in glory and lead His bride to the wedding day. When your thoughts centre around His coming, you will sing of it and speak of it. This will bring Him into your heart, and your love will increase.*

Your bridal love will be set aflame as you speak His name. The more a bride utters her Bridegroom's name, the more ardent her love will be. All day long and at night when you awake, say: "Jesus, Jesus, Jesus." This name contains the power to inflame the soul of the bride. Remember this always—there is virtue in pronouncing a name; but the greatest potency lies in calling upon the name of Jesus. When He hears His name, He lovingly inclines Himself. He will love the one who loves Him. You show your love when you speak the beloved's name with love.

Your bridal love will be deepened when you go aside with God. Only in times of quiet and solitude, when bride and Bridegroom are alone, can they give their complete love to each other. Only in a quiet place can they behold each other lovingly and speak lovingly. A fragile veil hangs over the lovers; their love is not displayed on the street, but rather in quiet and privacy. Seek, then, times of utter quietness when no one can disturb you, when everything around you is silent, when you are not distracted by anything else, when you can give yourself to Jesus completely; when you are all His. Believe that He will draw close to you. Believe that He is there, that He will speak to your heart. Only he who dares to go aside, and dares to pass through times of dryness will

* Basilea Schlink, *Lo! He Comes, Those Who Love Him* (Lakeland, 1969).

know the visitation of His love, and this will enhance the flame of love.

> *Only one thing do I desire:*
> *If it were mine,*
> *I would count all else as loss!*
> *God, to be evermore united with you,*
> *a loving sacrifice of your grace.*

R. A. Schroeder

Jesus and the Loving Soul

HIS PLEDGE:

I love you as no human being could possibly love you.

I give you everything you need.

I care for you as no human being could possibly care for you.

I do not let your sin stand in the way, for I love you, and I came to set sinners on the right path.

I tell you My most intimate thoughts, for you are My bride.

When you are joined to Me, nothing is too hard for you.

One day I will present you full of beauty before the Father.

HIS PLEA:

Let My love satisfy you.

Give Me your deepest love as you surrender your will to Me.

Let My eyes lead you.

Let all else be silent, so that I may speak.

Listen today for a desire of Mine.

Rest in My heart.

Bring Me joy by your adoration.

Proclaim Me, your Bridegroom, in every way you can contrive.

Be kind to your neighbour, and you will be kind to Me.

Think of Me often, that you may be inflamed with love.

Love Me in whatever form I may appear to you; love Me while I am working in you.

Love me as your Judge.

Love Me even in times of spiritual dryness; remain faithful to Me then.

Love Me by obeying Me in everyday life.

Meditate on My sufferings, and you will enter into My deepest heart.

Give Me your love as you come to love your cross.

HIS CHALLENGE:

If you wish to possess Me, choose My path of lowliness and disgrace.

If you wish to possess Me, no longer seek yourself and the fulfilment of your wishes, but rather the fulfilment of My will.

HIS PROMISE:

If you are in the wilderness, I would be everything to you.

If you are in darkness, I would be your Light.

If you are bound in sins, I would be your Redeemer.

If you are perplexed, I would be your Counsellor.

If you are sad, I would be your Laughter.

If you are fearful, take refuge in My love.

I will carry you through afflictions and tribulation.

Thus says the Lord,
I remember the devotion of your youth,
Your love as a Bride,
How you followed Me in the wilderness.

Jer. 2: 2

Jesus' Incomparable Love

Jesus' love is so intimate and blessed that He can bring utter bliss to His bride.

Jesus' love is so overflowing that He can overwhelm His bride with gifts.

Jesus' love is so attentive that He reacts to every wish and plea of His bride, and answers them—even when it does not seem so to us.

Jesus' love glows like a fire, so that it can set the bride's heart on fire again, if it has become indifferent, cold and lifeless.

Jesus' love is so radiant in its joy that it sheds its ray of joy upon the heart of the bride. It makes her happy and refreshes her when she is sad.

Jesus' love is so long-suffering that it never ceases to sustain the bride in all her sins and difficulties, He will support her all the way.

Jesus' love is so rich that it can fulfil all the bride's longings for love.

Jesus' love is individual; He loves His bride as though He had only this one bride on earth and could not live without her.

Jesus' love is full of tender sympathy. There is nothing that the bride suffers without her Bridegroom's knowledge and without His suffering it with her.

Jesus' love is patient. It can wait until the bride's heart is ready and her love mature for all that He demands.

Jesus' love is forgiving. It veils the bride's sins and inadequacies so that they can no longer be seen.

Jesus' love is a generous love. He gives His all to His bride so that she partakes of His very being and all He has.

Jesus' love is a perfect love. It lacks neither fire nor gentleness, neither strength nor tenderness, neither holiness nor intimate affection.

Jesus' love is heavenly love. It contains the whole bliss of heaven. Here on earth He imparts this love to His bride.

Jesus' love is a holy love which draws His bride to live in the realm of His holiness.

Jesus' love is so pure that He can never disappoint anyone, let alone His bride.

Jesus' love is so tender and understanding that He can understand and refresh His bride with His love even in her smallest anxieties and emotions.

*   *   *

. . . But what do I love, when I love You?

Not physical beauty, nor the glamour of the world, nor the shining bright light of day which is so pleasing to the eye; not sweet melodies of intricate songs, not manna and not honey; not the charm of love which attracts fleshly desires. These are not the things I love when I love You, my God.

And yet, I love You as though You were Light and sweet Scent and Melody and Food and the fulfilment of my spiritual desires! There inside my soul shines a Light which the world cannot comprehend; there melodies sound which cannot fade with time; there the sweet scents exhale a fragrance which no wind can disperse; . . . there laughs the happiness of united love which ever endures. All this is what I love when I love my God.   Augustine (354–430)

When the Bridegroom Comes

An experience in India: I wake at 2 a.m. I can hear loud music coming from the neighbouring village. It goes on until morning. What did this mean? At that time a bridegroom reached the village to fetch his bride. The whole village received him with music and joy. With a beating heart the bride waits for this moment, when the bridegroom comes to lead her to her new home, so that she may be always at his side.

All this is a parable, as everything earthly is a parable. What an hour it will be when Jesus comes as the Bridegroom!—and He will truly come one day. What melodies are sounding throughout heaven! What a company will welcome the Bridegroom when He returns with His bride to His heavenly home. His bride is waiting with a beating heart. She knows He is coming. Her whole heart eagerly awaits Him.

Can Jesus' bride on earth think of anything but His coming? Can she think of anything but His goodness and the life she will lead with Him? This will be the sum of all her thoughts because life with Jesus is the bride's portion. She can think of nothing else; she can wait for nothing else. She cannot aspire to anything but His coming. She must continually make for herself a picture of what life with Jesus will be like, the life that she will lead through all eternity at His side. Even when He takes His seat upon His throne as the most exalted King of all kings, she will not leave Him; rather, He will share His throne with her. She will sit on the throne with Him (Rev. 3: 21).

Has He not promised her that He will not judge the world by Himself, but will share this task with His bride (1 Cor. 6: 2)? She will judge the nations with Him (Rev. 2: 26–28). What a destiny awaits the soul that was a bride of the Lamb here on earth! But it is only the bride who will have the privilege of sharing the life of the Bridegroom in eternity.

Are you a bride of the Lamb? His bride shall inherit a blessed mystery. She has a blessed hope. She awaits a great and wonderful fulfilment. A bridal soul awaits the fulfilment of her highest longings and desires, and these will be bathed in the splendour of joy and delight. A bride has few needs, therefore, in this life. Am I a true bride of Jesus? How far does it still matter to me to be loved and esteemed by man, and to succeed in my work? How much do I care whether I am healthy or unhealthy, talented or untalented, loved or unloved? Only one thing should really matter to the bride: she has a Bridegroom, and this Bridegroom, Jesus, will come soon to take her home so that she may be joined to Him for ever.

This is her life. On this all her thoughts are centred. The Bridegroom is her Alpha and Omega; He is the Joy of her heart. She lives in the expectation of His coming. It is the love of the Bridegroom that makes her happy. All her thoughts centre upon her future life with Him.

Who is the bride of Jesus?—
Whoever is enthralled by Him, the one true Bridegroom, like the Apostle Paul, who always carried one name only in his heart, who spent himself only for the One, who waited only for the coming of the One: Jesus.

"Dearest Lord Jesus come soon to reign,"
Hear my voice pleading again and again,
"Come quickly, Lord," is the cry of Your bride,
I yearn to see You, and with You abide.

My heart is singing one ceaseless song,
"Jesus, my Bridegroom, why are You so long?
Come soon, come quickly, why do You delay?
I look and long for You, Lord, night and day."

The rapturous moment will come at last
The cry resounding, "The long wait is past!"
Jesus, the Bridegroom, will soon re-appear,
In love unite with the bride He holds dear.

Moment by moment I wait and yearn.
O won't You whisper when You will return?
My heart will leap then in love to Your side
O my Beloved, my Treasure and Pride.

WJ 14

Prudence as a Mark of the Bride

The Bridegroom came,
And those who were ready
Went in with Him
To the marriage feast!

Matt 25: 10

To nourish bridal love is to be watchful, always awake for Him, the Bridegroom. Blessed were the five virgins who were watchful in the midst of sleep! They were ready to meet the Bridegroom, to take part in the wedding. But how does the bride watch while sleeping so that she can hear the soft footsteps of her Bridegroom at midnight and be prepared to receive Him in this darkling hour?

Only through love, for love is immortal and cannot be destroyed nor can it sleep. So the heart of the bride wakes even when she sleeps. This love is divine; it is born of God. He first loved us, and poured this love into our hearts through the Holy Spirit.

Love abides in the heart of the bride of Jesus no matter what darkness may surround her and no matter how much the sleep may overcome her. This Love is like a sensitive instrument; if one string is plucked by the One whom she loves, it sounds and immediately the bride is awake. She rises quickly and rushes to meet Him. So she will never let slip the hour when her Bridegroom draws near to her; for her it is a foretaste of heaven. Certainly, then, she will not miss the hour when her Bridegroom comes again in glory to take His bride to Himself and celebrate the wedding with her.

If you long to be the bride of the Lamb, eager to meet the Bridegroom, then take care that this love lives within you. Do not let it fade. Keep it alive, so that you will be alert at His coming. If you have lost this divine life, then you will not wake at the midnight hour when sleep will have overcome all mankind and believers as well. Without this love you will not awake when He comes.

And behold, the Bridegroom will come soon. He is standing before the door! The hour of midnight is at hand, for love has already grown cold in many. Unrighteousness and lawlessness have gained the upper hand. People no longer respect God's commandments. The spirit of Antichrist is flooding the earth. It has enslaved men, so that they turn against God in hate and revolt, against every authority and order of life which He established. They turn with violence against those who still confess Jesus. The earth will become like hell.*

The midnight hour approaches. The signs Jesus gave for that time are being fulfilled. Hatred of Christ rages in the earth, and the persecution of Christians has reached unheard-of proportions. God's chosen people have returned to the land of their fathers. The gospel has been proclaimed throughout the world as a witness to the nations. Now a negative reaction has begun: in Christian countries men are falling away from the revelations which God made to them and from His commands. Everything proclaims that it is almost midnight. The Bridegroom is already on the way to meet His own. For whom will He open the door to the marriage-supper, that most blissful day of joy and of union between the bride and the Bridegroom? For whom will He open the door to the celebrations and exultations, the singing and rejoicing which will make the heavens resound? Only for those whose life is love for Jesus, the Bridegroom, will the door open.

Use what time is left. Open your heart wide so that the love for Jesus can stream in and guide your life, so that it fills you even while you are asleep, because you live only for Him. It is the last hour! Therefore, do not tolerate anything

* Basilea Schlink, *World in Revolt.*

which would hinder this love for Jesus, hatred for your fellow men, or false attachments to people or things through which Jesus might withdraw His love from you, and you might leave your first love. Do not tolerate anything which would draw you from His path of lowliness, of poverty, of disgrace, of obedience. Do not let yourself be tempted to follow paths which run according to earthly desires and which feed your ambitions, for this would hinder love for Jesus, and you would lose the first love.

So the hour will come when He whom your soul loves will appear. You will not realize this if you are not blazing with the first love. You will not be drawn by Him as by a magnet; only those who love will be drawn to the Bridegroom. In that hour it will be too late to open your heart that it may be filled anew with love for Jesus. You will not be able to buy any oil of love. It is now that your heart must be filled with this love. You must be a true bride so that He can recognize you when He comes to fetch His bride. He will recognize only those who loved Him ardently even in the darkest hour, and those whose lamp is filled with the oil of repentance and love. Only these will He recognize as His bride.

What a day of joy and delight, the wedding day of Jesus Christ, which He will celebrate with His bride, the bride of the Lamb while all heaven exults! It is worth sacrificing all you have to gain this love, this "pearl of great price". It is worth sacrificing everything to know the joy of this day. Yes, even if for the sake of this pearl of bridal love we give up everything on this earth that satisfies the body, soul and spirit, and everything that we yearn for, we have still given little for it. The Marriage of the Lamb—it is worth the sacrifice of everything to reach this high goal.

Therefore, know that the hour of midnight is here; the marriage is at hand. The Bridegroom is coming! Leave everything behind which would hinder you from going to meet Him! Live only to love Him!

The Spirit and the Bride say, "Come" . . .
He who testifies to these things says,
"Surely I am coming soon."
Amen. Come, Lord Jesus!

Rev. 22: 17, 20

THE HOLY HOUR IS COMING

The holy hour is coming,
When from the heav'nly throne
God's Son, who was incarnate
Will come to claim His own.

He waits with love expectant,
For His beloved bride,
Her life to Him she's given;
In bonds of love she's tied.

She hastens quickly to Him,
With joy and heav'nly bliss,
In ev'ry way preparing
To be completely His.

For through the blood of Jesus,
She now may walk in white,
Attain the heavenly wedding,
His realm of purest light.

The midnight hour is striking,
The dawn is now not far,
Awake! Watch with the faithful!
Soon shines the morning star.

Then you will share His splendour
Which like the sun will shine,
And enter then rejoicing
With Him the realm divine.

O live then for His Advent,
The trumpets glad declare,
To tell the bride He's coming,
The glorious day is here!

WJ 13

THERE IS ONE BESIDE ME

O there is One beside me now
And never will He leave my side,
And yet in heav'n He waits for me,
When home I come, His chosen bride.

Refrain
'Tis Jesus, only source of love,
My heav'nly Bridegroom from above.

Yes, He is always at my side,
Close, close beside me all the day;
We walk together hand in hand,
Together tread the self-same way.

There's One who loving comfort brings,
Who tenderly looks after me,
Who waits in love for my response
With yearning and expectancy.

There's One whom I can wholly trust,
For He has never failed me yet,
And when I need Him, He is there,
So all my hopes on His I set.

There's One who ever plans to bring
New joys, and endless bliss to me,
He cannot bear to see me sad,
In suff'ring or adversity.

There's One who knows my inmost heart,
The hidden causes of my fear,
He knows what most distresses me,
He sees and counts each secret tear.

There's One who by His own free will
Gave up His life to save my soul.
He snatched me from the jaws of hell,
Forgave my sins and made me whole.

There's One who suffers for my sake,
Yes, suffers endless pain for me,
So He transforms my pain and grief
And takes away my misery.

There's One who asks: "Do you love Me?"
And longs to hear me answer "Yes".
To gain my love He gave away
His life in utter selflessness.

There's One who as a beggar stands,
Beseeching me to give Him love.
Can I refuse and make Him sad
This suppliant Beggar for my love?

There's One who shows me all His heart,
Reveals the pain He has to bear
The wounds that sin inflict on Him.
And lets me in His suff'ring share.

There's One alone, yes, only One,
Who can with truth this promise give:
"For evermore I shall be yours,
  Because I live, you too will live."

Prayers

LOVE—THE MOST BEAUTIFUL CALLING

My dear Lord Jesus,

I thank You that You have created and redeemed me for love. I thank You that You have granted me, a sinner, the privilege of loving You out of repentance and gratitude for Your forgiveness.

Who is like You! I worship You. You are the fairest of the sons of men, the most precious treasure in heaven and on earth, the bright sun of my life, the joy of my heart!

Teach me to love You as you are worthy to be loved, You who laid down Your life for me out of love. Nourish the spark of love in my heart with the flame of Your love, for You first loved me. Your love seeks to give me the most precious gift; an intimate, fervent love for You so that I might return Your love.

I thank You that You have appointed me the most wonderful calling: to love You as my Lord and Bridegroom with all my heart and with all my strength. That makes me utterly happy and gives purpose and fufilment to my life.

For love's sake, my Lord Jesus, I want to tread Your path with You. I do not want to forsake You. I want to give You my answer of love in deeds. I want to take up my cross and follow You on Your path. I want to lose my life for You in sacrifice, renunciation, obedience and self-humiliation. Amen.

THANKSGIVING FOR HIS UNSPEAKABLE GRACE

Our dear Lord Jesus,

We thank You for the indescribable gift of being able to

love You, because You love us. How unworthy we are! How many others seek love and happiness and do not find it! Yet, we have all our joy in You, because You, Lord Jesus, contain all joy. We may drink of the spring of Your love. We are surrounded with love by the Lord of all lords; we are never alone. We may do everything together with You; we may always be at Your side; we are drawing close to the time when we shall be united with You for ever.

How can we thank You that You are a Bridegroom for us human beings, You who are the King of all kings, Lord of the whole world and of the companies of angels! You have chosen us sinners and have come down to us in love. You have made a covenant with us. You have revealed Yourself to us as Bridegroom by giving Yourself entirely to us, by loving us with an inexpressible love. Everything that is Yours now belongs to us also. Who can fathom such wealth and such bliss? We worship and adore You.   Amen.

LET ME BE YOUR BRIDE COMPLETELY

My Lord Jesus,

How can I thank You for wooing me, an unworthy soul? How can I thank You for choosing me to be Your bride?

Let me be Your bride completely: preoccupied with Your love, consumed in Your love, lavishing myself on You in love. In You I shall see all the beauty of heaven and earth. In You I shall always have my home and only in You. You alone are sufficient for me.

Grant that I may be Your bride completely. Let me be surrounded by Your love. Let me draw close to You. Let me be sustained by Your strong arm, which created and redeemed the world. I would be weak, faint and helpless so that You, my Bridegroom, may give me Your richness that is full of rejoicing. As Your bride I confess again and again that I am a sinner. I want to find my refuge in Your wounds, which were opened for me, a sinner.

I thank You that You have called Your bride to love and again to love. Make me a lover, a true lover, one who gives himself completely to You. Make me a lover who for love of You will embrace every sacrifice, who can share Your innermost heart, and the fellowship of Your sufferings.

Grant me this through Your grace. Amen.

HUMBLY RECEIVING THE "BEGGAR FOR LOVE"

Our dear Lord Jesus,

We bow down deeply before You and humble ourselves, because You had to become a "Beggar for love". How often we have refused to admit You, how often we have let You stand out in the cold when You knocked! We humble ourselves and acknowledge that You have often found our hearts so unready to receive You, because we were not willing to choose You alone. Time and again we have put other things before You.

Yet, You have laid down Your life for us. You have loved us more than tongue can declare. So we beseech You: Show us what it is that fills our hearts, what sways our heart so that we cannot put You first of all. Then let us bring that idol to You; let us renounce it and claim Your victory over it. Let us see Your superior power, and know that You delivered us that we might belong to You.

You desire our love, because You yearn for Your bride. You long to take up Your abode in a heart that has made room for You. You are happy when we commit ourselves to You, when we drive out all the idols from our lives so that Your love might reign in us. May You no longer be disappointed with us, but may You receive comfort and joy.

Take our hearts, our wishes and desires and all our time—may everything be at Your disposal. We have but one desire—that in our hearts You may find the response to Your love. Amen.

A PLEA FOR MORE LOVE

Our Lord Jesus,

We thank You that You desire our love and that we can make You happy when we tell You: "I love You. I want to be with You and to live only for You, and for your concerns."

We pray for one thing only: Help us to love You more! You find so few among those who belong to You who really love You beyond all else, who really love You with their whole heart. You are a Sun of love, filled with the power of love. Therefore, we beseech You, direct the glowing stream of love into our hearts.

We are Yours. Grant us a consuming love for You. Let us, moved by this love, fulfil our work for You in the world. In Your love the world can be remade.

This love cannot be withstood for it is fed by Yours. Grant us this love! There is nothing like it.   Amen.

A PRAYER FOR DESERT TIMES

My Lord Jesus,

If only I have You, let my flesh and my heart fail, but I shall not be moved. I shall not fear, for You are with me, Jesus, my Bridegroom.

And though a host encamp against me, You will remain the comfort and portion of my heart. You are strong and mighty. Have You not conquered hell? Must not every enemy bow before You? You are truly Lord, even over all that would oppress me. Are You not He who created heaven and earth? "This is my beloved, and this is my friend"—what shall I fear? I shall rest upon You and my soul will be restored. Comforted, I shall pass through all my times of dryness through all the threats of the enemy; for I am joined to You, and nothing is stronger than the fellowship of love. You can transform desert ways into the fields of paradise, for You are there and You refresh my soul. Yes, and You will also make me able to help others who are desert-bound, with the comfort of Your love. I thank You, Lord! Amen.

A PLEA FOR THE PROVING OF
LOVE IN SUFFERING

Our dear Lord Jesus,

Your love is stronger than death. Therefore, we pray one prayer: Grant us this strong love so that we may not deny You in the hour of trial. Make us strong in You by strengthening our love.

Help us to practise the small sacrifices of every day so that we shall be able to offer You our whole lives as a sacrifice in the hour of trial. Make us strong to love You only and not to prize other things. You know how lesser things still engross us, the sufferings of the body and the soul. You know we fear that we may not endure if we are made to choose between our bodily safety and our witness to Your name, if it should even mean martyrdom.

Therefore, once more we beseech You: Fill us with the mighty stream of Your love that we may not disappoint You in our hour of trial, but rather fill Your heart with joy and gratitude, so that You can say: "How sweet is your love, my sister, my bride!" (Song of Solomon 4: 10).   Amen.

DEDICATION

Make me strong and firm, burning with love, burning with dedication for You and hard as granite, with the one aim only:
I want Jesus, nothing but Jesus—

I want no relief of any hardship; I do not want the comfort of seeing and feeling—

120

I want only to embrace You in faith and love You, Jesus—
in darkness and temptation.

Mother Martyria.

May nothing be dearer to me than You,
may nothing concern me more than You,
may nothing but Your sufferings cause me to mourn,
may nothing but You elate my heart,
may nothing make me sad but Your sufferings for my sins.
You alone are the One upon whom are centred my thoughts,
*   feelings, wishes and desires*
Jesus, Jesus, Jesus—only You!

*   *   *

Christ, to Thee my life belongeth,
All I have and all I own
Place I at Thy sole disposal
For Thy use and Thine alone.

Thou hast time and strength provided.
Talents equal to my state,
So to Thee with all my being
Ev'ry day I dedicate.

Loving Thee is all I live for,
I would spend my life for Thee,
All my will to Thee surrendered.
All I do bring praise to Thee.

I would give Thee, sweet Lord Jesus,
What is precious, dear to me,
Then Thyself to me Thou givest,
And Thy love transfigures me.

Thou, O Christ, art my sole Passion,
Thou the Source of all my joy;
Back to Thee thy gifts I render,
For Thee all my powers employ.

*   *   *

Dearest Beloved, O Jesus, my King,
Precious the gift Thou, my Bridegroom dost bring,
Streaming through heaven with glory divine,
Perfect in beauty—and yet Thou art mine.

Sweet is Thy Life Thou givest to me.
Deep in Thy heart do I sink lovingly;
Lavish on Thee all the love of my heart,
Give to Thee all, so beloved Thou art.

Blissful the joy I find always in Thee,
More than all grief that Thy will brings to me
All I hold dear shall my sacrifice be,
This is the dowry I offer to Thee.

Take what I offer, my wishes fulfil,
Take all I treasure, my freedom of will;
Take those I love most, my country and home,
Take what I live for and claim as my own.

Dearest Beloved, my offering see,
All that brings comfort or pleasure to me;
Nothing is dearer, more precious than Thee,
Thou art my life, and my Crown Thou shalt be.

*   *   *

Lord, You deserve that men forget
All earthly things for love of You
That men should give their all and let
Their hearts be wholly merged in You.
Yes, You deserve all this, O Lord.

Lord, You deserve that tears bedew
My earthly way, my whole life through.
My Spouse, I will stay close by You
Yes, You deserve, Lord, all my love.

*   *   *

O none can be loved as is Jesus
None like His is found anywhere.
'Tis He whom I love, whom I live for,
For no one with Him can compare.

I follow now close in His footsteps
The path that He trod here below,
I only desire what He gives me,
And only His way I will go.

My heart is at peace and so joyful,
For all I desire He supplies.
I look now for nothing but Jesus,
Who all of my hopes satisfies.

WJ 219

ABIDING WITH JESUS TO COMFORT HIM

Jesus, Jesus, my Beloved,
Lamb of God now glorified,
Once You chose the cross of suff'ring,
Willingly for us You died.
Let me, Lord, with love now follow
In Your way of pain and death,
Let me feel the grief and anguish
Which You felt at ev'ry step.

Jesus, Jesus, my Beloved,
How I worship and adore
All the loving, willing suff'ring
Which You in Your passion bore.
Let me trace Your stumbling footsteps
As You bow beneath the cross,
Let me now my whole life offer
Which You won at such great cost.

So I now Your cross approaching
With the worship that is due,
Son of God, in holy splendour,
All my love I give to You,
Using it to laud and honour
In a thousand, thousand ways,
My Belovéd and my Sov'reign,
Jesus, worthy of all praise.

*   *   *

Jesus, Lord, to love You only,
I shall live for this alone,
To Your heart some comfort bringing,
All Your suff'ring making known.

Naught I care now for my troubles
Since I've seen Your pain and loss,
To console You all my longing,
Willingly take up my cross.

May my heart now burn within me
For Your grief and agony,
Leading men to heed Your suff'ring,
And Your comforters to be.

WJ 231

*   *   *

With all my heart I shout and sing:
I am the bride of Christ the King!
To know His love He chose me.

My heart exults, with joy it springs.
And of sweet Jesus ever sings,
My heart's belovèd Sov'reign.

So I must love Him, only Him,
My heart and soul are drawn to Him,
Him will I love for ever.

ADORATION OF THE BRIDEGROOM

Who makes as happy, Jesus, as You,
Therefore my heart rejoices in You,
Jesus, O Joy Eternal!

Jesus, my well-spring of joy ever new,
Heaven's great joy to us comes through You,
Jesus, O Joy Eternal.

You create joy when hearts let You in
For You cleanse guilt, and blot out all sin,
Jesus, O Joy Eternal.

Kingdom of heaven shall truly begin
Where sinners are repenting of sin,
Jesus, O Joy Eternal.

Jesus, my Lord, my God and my King,
You fill my heart with praises to sing—
Jesus, O Joy Eternal.

Jesus, my joy-spring so deep and so broad,
Joy on this earth You've richly outpoured,
But O the joy when we see You!

WJ 221

*   *   *

I sing aloud: "Who can with You compare
Here on the earth, in heaven, or anywhere?"
No, none with You, Lord Jesus, can compare,
And none Your splendid glory ever share.
                    Who is like You?

I sing aloud: I sing of One alone,
His is the name that ever in me sounds.
O Jesus, Jesus, I am all Your own.
I am Your bride, my praise for You abounds,
                    To give You joy.

I sing aloud: No, like You, there is none.
I find in You my joy for evermore.
A myriad times more glorious than the sun,
While myriad myriads worship and adore
                    My Lord most dear.

I sing aloud: Your majesty I praise,
For I am Yours, the one You chose as Bride,
Who knows Your heart and all Your loving ways,
And shares Your joy and sorrow at Your side
                    With pride and love.

WJ 236

ADORATION OF THE HEAVENLY GLORY OF JESUS

What grace is given me
Thy beauteous face to see!
Near Thee to dwell always.
Like sweet celestial wine
Drinks in this soul of mine
Thy loveliness, O Christ.

No one Thy peer may be,
All beauty pales 'fore Thee,
O loveliness divine!
Thou heav'nly splendour art
And so my human heart
In rapturous love is plunged.

Beside Thee I will stay,
Keep step with Thee alway;
I'll leave Thee nevermore,
My love doth me constrain
Close by Thee to remain,
To work and rest in love.

Blissful the life of grace
Sinners may now embrace,
Consumed with love for Thee,
Quenched then our souls' deep thirst,
In bliss each heart immersed,
Love cannot lead astray.

WJ 232

*   *   *

O Countenance of most holy beauty!
O Countenance, so full of God's eternal peace!
O Countenance of our peerless Sovereign!
O Countenance more dazzling than the brightest sun,
How divine, how fair are You!
All Your features mirror traits of the divine nature in an ineffable and eternal majesty.
Out of You there came all the glories of creation on which the light of Your countenance always shines.
Out of You there came also all the beauty and dignity of human nature,
For every expression of love is found united in Your countenance, Lord Jesus Christ.
You are enthroned above the cherubim, above all worlds.
You are the Prince of supernatural beings, full of divine power.

If Your countenance should show displeasure, all earthly power and glory lose their attraction.

To me it is granted to see in You the traits of the divine nature.

O what bliss of love! I will remain here for ever.

Only one thing could fill my heart with such delight through all eternity!

Only one theme there is on which I could sing for ever!

Your countenance of most holy beauty!

Before it all heaven stands hushed in silent worship.

Your countenance!

How sweetly sounds the music of the harps!

Through highest heaven the angels sing their songs of praise in honour of Your countenance which is so holy and so divinely fair.

And heaven itself is illumined by the light of Your countenance and is bathed in its beauty.

Your countenance shines with ceaseless immeasurable love.

The whole earth was saved by the vision of Your countenance.

It heals and refreshes and draws God's children home to their Father's house.

It is filled with an eternal beauty and a wondrous splendour.

The beauty of Your countenance holds my whole heart captive.

*   *   *

O Jesus, clad right royally,
With shining crown of majesty,
O Sovereign due all honour!
As Bridegroom splendid, grand and fair,
Who can on earth with You compare,
Attain Your peerless beauty?

A thousand suns were ne'er so bright
As is the radiance of Your light,
The radiance of Your glory.
O noble face, so pure and fair
Only in worship angels dare
To look on Love so perfect.

The whole world shouts with joy and pride
Around Your throne where waits the bride
In wedding robe exultant.
O Spouse, so splendid, noble now
Your chosen bride You will endow
With equal grace and splendour.

*   *   *

WJ 241

Jesus! Name all heav'n is singing!
Name with which all heav'n is ringing,
Throbbing with exultant joy!
You are throned in splendour glorious,
Crowned with crowns of beauty wondrous
More than man can comprehend.

Jesus! Heaven's joy and wonder,
Shining like the sun in splendour!
Jesus! Name most sweet to hear!
Angels all-adoring name You,
As their Sovereign Lord acclaim You,
As their God and Maker own.

Listen to the voices swelling,
One by one they keep re-telling,
Tidings of dear Jesu's name.
Heav'n with that sweet name is ringing
Countless choirs its glory singing,
Sound the praise of His great love

Jesus! Glorious name resplendent,
Ev'ry bliss and joy transcendent
Dwells within Your heart of love.
Heaven kneels in awe adoring,
Whispers softly of the glory
Of Your love and majesty.

WJ 240

ADORATION OF THE SUFFERING SAVIOUR

The angel choirs are singing,
And sinners praises bringing
To Christ, the Lamb of God.
As love its homage proffers,
Its purest anthems offers
The Lamb enthroned in highest heav'n.

Love now will hymn His glory,
Will tell again the story
The great thing He has done.
Love can be silent never,
But in new ways for ever
Proclaim to all our Jesu's praise.

Love is forever singing
And thanks to Jesus bringing,
How He salvation won.
Love praises Him who suffered,
That we might joy be offered,
That endless joy at God's right hand.

Love praises, yet bewailing
That men their God are nailing
On to the cross of pain.
Love praises His strong patience,
His bearing all in silence,
To pay our debts to save our souls.

Fervent indeed the praises
The ransomed earth now raises
In many thousand ways.
They give God endless glory,
Recount redemption's story,
As on the cross the Saviour dies.

O joy beyond expressing!
Now dawns that day of blessing
When all the Lamb will praise.
Lo, hear God's children bringing
Their grateful praise, and singing
The hymn of glory to the Lamb.

WJ 89

Testimonies from Canaan

THE SUN HAS SCORCHED ME (Song of Solomon 1: 6)

After serving abroad for several years, I was permitted to return home from the "desert" to Canaan. In the "desert" I had been deprived of many of the blessings of fellowship, and I looked forward to returning to a spiritual abundance. But in spite of the abundance I felt cold and unresponsive. I found this very strange and sad; I began to pity myself. After a while I realized that there was something which barred the way to Jesus' heart. What had happened?

When I was sent out to Jerusalem I found it very hard to leave Canaan. To obey was sheer sacrifice. This changed insensibly as time went on. My work began to give me satisfaction; it was no longer entirely sacrifice. I did not observe that I had become the centre of my service; I had grown satisfied and sure of myself. My service had become busyness, and profited nothing.

Then I understood that Jesus' judgment had been spoken against me: "I have somewhat against thee, because thou hast left thy first love. Remember therefore from whence thou art fallen, and repent" (Rev. 2: 4, 5, AV). The "eye salve" (Rev. 3: 18) which brought me this recognition was at first very painful; but as soon as I had fully accepted this verdict and had humbled myself, the barrier fell which had separated me from Him. I began to weep and rejoice and worship Him all at the same time. A new love began. His presence was tangibly there. It cannot be described in words.

Again, repentance was the gateway to a new bridal love for Jesus. Time and again I have experienced that repentance enables me to discover who I am and how overwhelming He is, and how much He is to be loved.

Sister of Mary Caecilie

I SOUGHT HIM (Song of Solomon 3: 2).

In the winter of 1959 I often spent many pleasurable hours playing the church organ in Brevik, Norway. It was wonderful to be abroad for the first time, and it was marvellous to be an organist, even though my main purpose was to learn how to cook! I loved music more than anything else and had just passed my examinations in church music. It was a gay and carefree time, which I enjoyed to the full. To be sure, my life had belonged to Jesus since I was a child. I loved Him, but my love had not led me to unquestioning discipleship.

I could not really say how it happened, but one evening, as I finished practising on the organ, I had an irresistible urge to commit my life to Jesus, to give Him everything. Although I was on my way out of the church I went back, and in the empty sanctuary I sang

> Lord, my Shepherd, Fount of all joys,
> Thou art mine, and I am Thine,
> No one can part us . . .
> Let me, let me reach the place,
> Where we eternally each other embrace.

With the strange certainty that my prayer would be answered, I departed to the small village nearby where I was living.

Two hours later, on the same evening, I was on my way to a friend's house. A bright red glow in the sky had a strange effect upon me. A child ran by and shouted to me in Norwegian: "The church is burning!" I did not understand a word, but I ran the rest of the way up the hill and saw Brevik church immersed in a sea of flame. (I learned later that a defect in the heating system had caused the fire.) All I remember is that I sank down on my knees into the snow convicted by the holiness of God, and prayed for His mercy. It was not only the shock of seeing God's house on fire, but I realized that all my organ music, collected over the years, and all my other possessions from singing manuals to metronome were going up in smoke before my eyes.

Jesus, who knew that my heart was divided, showed me in a flash the truth about myself. He showed me the difference between pious deception and reality. In that moment I was freed from my preoccupation with music, and understood that one cannot have Jesus as dearest Lord without giving up all things for Him. But since then I have discovered what an incomparable exchange this is, how trivial is the worth of what we have forsaken compared with the inexpressible wealth of what we have gained.

Sister of Mary Justina

HE COMFORTS ME WITH FLOWERS

On the day of my bridal consecration as a Sister of Mary, someone gave me a stem of mimosa bearing the inscription: "May I love my Bridegroom Jesus with a love as tender and sensitive as the mimosa."

Many years later, I accompanied Mother Basilea to the Sinai Peninsula. Here God had offered His eternal covenant of love. A pain shot through my heart: my life made no response at all to that love. Could the covenant that He made with me on the day of my bridal consecration still possibly be valid? On the same day a man who was working as a photographer on Mount Sinai brought me a bunch of mimosa. He just wanted to share his joy at having found such flowers on Sinai, which is primitive rock, almost without vegetation. In a flash I recognized the sign, and who it was who had really given the flowers to me.

A few years later on the anniversary of my bridal consecration I was in Norway. Constant demands were made upon me and I was greatly in need of some refreshment and restoration. I thought: "My Lord Jesus, are You hiding Yourself from me so much, because I have disappointed You?" Tired out, I returned to my hotel and heaved a sigh when I learned that someone wanted to see me. But this lady, whom I did not know, merely wanted to give me some flowers. *It was mimosa!* His love forgets nothing.

Sister of Mary Benedicta

It had been a long, hard day working in the laundry. Secretly I was wishing for a quiet evening of meditation, since I was so tired; but it happened to be my turn to do the washing up! We had had a festive meal with trimmings. More than a hundred people were there and the pots and pans from lunch and dinner were stacked high.

Then those two little words, which Mother Basilea had given us out of her own experience for such times came to my help. She had taught us to say aloud or to ourselves over and over again: "For You Jesus!", and these words were a comfort to me as I stood at the sink and could hear the cheerful noise from the dining hall. There were guests that evening. Those two words were a sure shield against all the enemy's arrows of self-pity.

But not only so. Jesus Himself answered me! When I got to my room that evening and shut the door behind me, it was as though someone was actually there—someone who stood beside me and greeted me lovingly. Suddenly a sentence rang through my heart: "I come to My beloved as dew on a flower!" I was surprised at this and puzzled as to where I could have heard or read that sentence. Then there was a knock at the door. The mothers had asked a Sister to bring me a bowl of flowers, with a verse which spoke of love for Jesus. Pleased and surprised I thought: "Is that it—'I come to My beloved as dew on a flower'?"

As I knelt by my bed, too tired to make my own prayers, I reached for an old prayer book. I could scarcely believe my eyes as my glance fell upon the words: "I come to My beloved as dew on a flower." It was as though Jesus sought to emphasize this once more: "Do you now believe that I am here, that I want to come to you?"

I imagine that few people that evening were as happy as I was.

Sister of Mary Mechthild

HE RAISES UP THE POOR FROM THE DUST
   (1 Sam. 2: 8)

I remember going through a very difficult time, which my sins deservedly brought upon me. But at that time I understood as I never had before who Jesus is and how wonderful is His love for a sinner. Instead of turning away from the faithless, he comforts them!

One can often feel very much alone in a dark hour, even when the kindest people are there. At such times Jesus Himself seemed to be standing beside me. His love surrounded me, and I had the triumphant assurance: "I have Him!" Those three words had such a mysterious power that they tore me out of the deeps and filled me suddenly with a blissful security.

When my troubles started, the Lord gave me this verse: "He raises up the poor from the dust . . ." (1 Sam. 2: 8). This is almost the same as Psalm 113: 7 which appears in the Sunday vesper, and for many weeks, as I sang that verse, I held it to my heart and cherished it as a personal treasure. At times when my sin seemed to overcome me, so that I could not imagine what would happen to me, Jesus would in a moment cause this verse to shine brightly for me and come close to me in His royal sovereignty of love. Does it not become Him as Bridegroom—and Him alone—in His own time to raise the poor from the dust? He does not yield to another His rights as a bridegroom. So I was never left in the poverty of poor human thinking, but simply abandoned to His loving wisdom.

A Sister of Mary

HE CARED FOR HIM (Deut. 32: 10)

Pleasant surprises are very welcome, especially when they are unexpected. But unpleasant surprises are a different thing—the less expected, the bigger the shock, and the more they hurt. Of recent years we have noticed in the Bible studies how tenderly Jesus sought to prepare His disciples for the time of His sufferings, so that they might not be shattered when it came.

I remember walking down the street, my mind busy with ordinary things. Then it seemed as though someone was knocking tenderly and carefully on the door of my heart. Suddenly I knew: "Something very difficult is going to happen. Everything will depend on how you take it."

Later the same evening something I had forgotten for years came back to my mind and hit me at my most sensitive point. Looking back at it, I suddenly felt tremendously guilty. Despair threatened me deeper than I had ever known; the situation seemed beyond me. Then I remembered the Lord's word: ". . . It will all depend on how you take it", and in that moment I said to myself "The God who warned you about this is ready to absolve this guilt and cancel the consequences of it!"

Sister of Mary Benedicta

DRAW ME AFTER YOU,
LET US MAKE HASTE (Song of Solomon 1: 4)

Jesus has a special way of asking for our love. God does not ask us for our "I will" as One who promises good things and shields us from all difficult ones. His greatest attraction, which wins a human soul for bridal love and calls that soul to follow Him on His way, lies in His sufferings.

Among us there is a young Sister from Arizona. What brought her to this small Land of Canaan near Darmstadt in Germany? Her father and her brother are pilots. She herself had planned to become a teacher. She had only vague thoughts about Jesus, but one evening everything changed. In the night, between Maundy Thursday and Good Friday, as she meditated with our Sisters in Phoenix on Jesus' Passion Way, she realized for the first time what He had undergone for her sins, for love's sake. She worshipped Him as the Man of Sorrows and could only ask: "How can I thank

Thee for Thy love?" And then she understood that she could thank Him only by giving Him her whole life.

Sister of Mary Ruth

LOOK AND SEE IF THERE IS
ANY SORROW LIKE MY SORROW (Lam. 1: 12)

The "Garden of Jesus' Sufferings" on Canaan testifies to all that he suffered for love of us. Many visitors have found God in this garden. They have wept tears of repentance; they have accepted their sufferings. They have heard the call of God; they have begun to feel a new and fervent love for Jesus. We can bear witness to this.

So many guests on Canaan have told us that the most decisive and the most precious hours of the retreat were the ones they spent in the Garden of Jesus' Sufferings.

A young girl from Scandinavia spent an hour there one afternoon. The picture of the despised and forsaken Lord, crowned with His crown of thorns, brought about the turning point of her life. Thereupon she gave up everything: her home, her promising education, her desire for marriage and a family, to take instead a place of lowliness and obedience to Jesus—and that in a country which had committed such grievous crimes against her own.

A young man whom, it seemed, counselling could not help suddenly found, in the sight of the sufferings of Jesus, the way back from rebellion to commitment.

At one point in the history of our Sisterhood when the slanderous attacks against our Mothers had begun again, we fell into self-pity. One of us finally put this self-pity into words: "And there is no one who can defend you . . ." In a brief but pithy word, Mother Basilea immediately replied: "Have you forgotten the Garden of Sufferings? the picture of Jesus standing alone before the court? What do you think it is there for?" That brief answer was more effective than a dozen sermons.

A Sister of Mary

FOLLOW IN THE TRACKS OF THE FLOCK
   (Song of Solomon 1: 8)

For a long time I had realized that a Jewish friend of mine was seeking Jesus and wanted to know about Him. When the frontiers were open to her after the Six Day War, her great longing to visit the Holy Places of Jesus, and especially His Passion Way, could be fulfilled. We scarcely spoke about it, but I understood that the secret word of Jesus, the Bridegroom, was leading her into His presence.

Months passed. Had anything come of this encounter with the Passion Way of Jesus? I met her again and learned that she had known great suffering. Serious and slanderous insinuations and accusations had been made against her. She was by nature a very lively and energetic person; at home and at work everything seemed to pivot upon her, but she told me of these things calmly, without reproaching anyone. She must have seen my thoughts for she said quietly: "How could I have defended myself against their words? I had the privilege of standing with Jesus. He was innocent, but He received all their slanders in silence—for my sake. This was something that I could do for Him."

What a glad moment for Jesus! Someone trod His path out of love for Him—one of His chosen people.

A Sister of Mary

SING ALOUD ... O DAUGHTER OF
JERUSALEM (Zeph. 3: 14)

Often, when we talk to people who come to Canaan or when we lecture elsewhere someone asks what we actually do! When we begin, very happily, to answer this question there are one or two points where we hesitate for words, because it is not easy for people unacquainted with Canaan's inner spiritual commission to understand. We are not willing to submit these tasks and duties to the yard-stick of social profitability. The ministry on the Mount of Olives in Jerusalem is of this kind.

"Sing, wherever you are and wherever you go," said Mother Basilea when she left us in 1962. She left three of us behind on the Mount of Olives in this new little settlement, which God had so wonderfully prepared for us. And sing we did. People said that we must come from a singing order. The ministry among the poor, among the tourists and among the pilgrims grew greatly while we were there. Yet the deepest reason for our being sent may be seen in the words of the following letter:

". . . Oh, if only the songs of love and thanksgiving would fill Jerusalem, and those who love Jesus would cease to be silent! The Holy Places of Jesus and the Via Dolorosa are filled with noise, dirt, clamour, commotion and commercialism. How sad it is to hear the muezzins cry out day and night from the minarets to remind the faithful of the greatness of Mohammed and of their prayer duties, while the Christians are silent! Who will dedicate his life so that Jesus may receive love and adoration here? Who will help call people to make some sacrifice in order to make a pilgrimage to the Holy Land? Our Lord seeks pilgrims who will sing and praise Him, who will declare how worthy He is to be loved and adored in the midst of a heathen and unbelieving world . . ."

Sisters of Mary Caecilie and Elisabeth,
Beit Gaudia, Mount of Olives

WHY THIS WASTE? (Matt. 26: 28)

On both of the occasions when we sought to build a chapel of praise in Switzerland, we were in a poor financial position. One of the reasons we had so little money was that we had just built a Herald Chapel on Canaan (Darmstadt, West Germany) that could seat a thousand people. Now why should we spend so much on a chapel in Switzerland? The people who lived there did not want it. Not even our friends could understand what it was for.

The building costs were much exaggerated by rumours. A Swiss lady took her questions to her minister. Whom did such a building serve? What use was it? Surely the money could have been better used. She told us later—that her minister said, "Well a lot is being done for our people. We have hardly any poor left. But who is ready to do anything for the glory of God? Shouldn't we give Him something for once?" That is the way "first love" thinks. But apart from that, much counselling help has been given at these places to spiritually exhausted visitors.

Sister of Mary Myrrhia

ALL FOR HIM

Towards the end of my summer vacation on Canaan my heart was burning with the question: How shall I serve my Lord Jesus for the rest of my life? It was just before my last semester at college, and I was really set on finishing my studies for a doctorate in physics. Plans for further experimental studies in nuclear physics were whirling around in my head, since two professors had already given me a wonderful opportunity to do research with them in this field. Physics was the joy of my life, the love of my life—almost everything I ever thought about had to do with physics.

But in the previous year Jesus had drawn me out of my atheistic way of thinking into a new life. While I studied the Scriptures during my summer on Canaan one thing deeply troubled me: God's continual cry that we do not love Him enough. Many questions filled my heart: Could I offer Him in ordinary life the love He so much longs for? Or should I perhaps begin some sort of ministry among students while still working on physics? Or again, should I give up all my studies and plans in physics and become a parish minister? What of marriage? If I did turn from physics, would my family and friends approve or even understand? In a word—what was my service to be for my Lord Jesus?

With all this on my mind I asked for advice while I was still on Canaan. The answer was quite clear: "Seek *Jesus*, only Jesus. He will show you the next step and the one after that, if you seek *Him* alone. Spend no more time going over the various possibilities—just spend time with Him." It was also suggested that I should spend much of my time in quiet and in serious prayer about all this.

The following week I returned to the U.S.A. to begin the autumn semester—still without any definite leading. But I did not give up hope, for He had promised: "Blessed is the man who makes the Lord his trust" (Psalm 40: 4). As time went on, some doors closed, and others opened. But then, quite suddenly the Lord showed me that I had continually forsaken Him. Instead of loving Him with my whole heart, I had lavished my love and time on other people and other things. My eyes were opened, and in a moment everything was clear. I knew that I must give up everything for Jesus, according to His Word—even my family and home, my country and all that went with it; and now it was not difficult at all, because *He* is worth more than anything else in the world. He had become my greatest Joy and my only Love. Physics just does not begin to compare with Jesus! He is my heavenly Bridegroom, the Source of all love and joy, not just for this life, but for all eternity.

I wanted to leap and sing out of love for Jesus, that He had called me to such a life—to consecrate my whole life to Him in this way. What tremendous love! and in his tender love the Lord later confirmed for me this new way of life with a verse of Scripture given to me at the festival of my investiture as a Canaan Franciscan Brother:

"As the bridegroom rejoices over the bride,
so shall your God rejoice over you" (Isa. 62: 5).
Canaan Franciscan Brother Silvestro

A GARDEN INCLOSED IS MY SISTER
   (Song of Solomon 4: 12 AV)

The verse from the Psalms which prophetically pronounces the lamentation of our suffering Lord: "I looked ... for comforters" (Psalm 69: 20) pierced deeply into my heart as a young Sister of Mary. But who can comfort Jesus? Only one who is deeply concerned with His agony and suffering—even with His suffering today; only one who can forget his own suffering. Time and again I wrote this prayer in my diary, that I might become a true comforter of Jesus, one who might console Him and bring joy to His heart.

But in reality my life was not like this. In the Sisterhood of Mary it is the custom that the younger Sisters go not only to one of the Mothers for spiritual counselling but should also have the opportunity of going to one of the more mature Sisters who is assigned to her. It was quite natural that I should do this when I entered a period of spiritual dryness, but often I sensed in periods of spiritual night that Jesus wanted me to forego such comfort for His sake. Usually I was too weak to do this.

Once when I was on the verge of despair because I seemed to fail every day, I wanted to speak to my Sister. However she was extremely busy, and had many responsibilities. In my egoistic way I reacted hypersensitively, feeling that she was not as friendly and sympathetic as usual. Soon afterwards the Spirit of God opened my eyes and showed me how anxious I was to be understood, loved and considered. I mourned, with tears of true repentance because I had been inconsiderate towards my "Sister", but more important than that, I now mourned that so often I had forgotten Jesus and had been concerned only with my own interests. I had sought comfort for myself; I had not been a comforter to Him.

I could think of one thing only: "Go in the quietness to Him! Tell Him everything!" I knew just what I must do. I must confess my failures calmly to my Sisters wherever this

needed to be done, without self-pity because of my un-
fortunate disposition. Every burden I took to Him alone. It
was ten days before Christmas that the Spirit of God spoke
to me, and that Christmas I experienced more grace than
ever before. He granted me His presence. I could spend hours
in prayer alone with Him, desiring nothing else. All I wanted
was to tell Him everything.

Sister of Mary Salome

I HAVE SOMEWHAT AGAINST THEE ...
   (Rev. 2: 4 AV)

Quite early in my life I loved Jesus only. For love of Him I
had joyfully sacrificed everything: home, expectations,
parents and friends. I followed Him and devoted my life to
serving Him. I knew how wonderful it is when Jesus
"knocks on the door" and how wonderful it is to hasten to
let Him in. But a human soul, even when it seems to have
given up everything to follow the way of unquestioning
discipleship, can still at heart be seeking its own advantages,
and to please itself. Sometimes its desire is for spiritual enjoyment.

This was made plain to me one day in a way that absolutely convicted me. The truth was clear to me: I want the
enjoyment of bridal love, but not the Jesus Himself who
says: "If a man loves me, he will keep my word." Although
His Word said: "Humble yourselves before the Lord!" this
was just what I had not done. I rebelled against Him and no
longer loved Him; I complained, and like the servant in the
parable I thought, "God is a hard man. He demands what He
has not given" (Matt. 25: 24). This I thought of God and this I
experienced. My work was not blessed; I was restless, and I
could not concentrate. Even in prayer my rebellious
thoughts pursued me. For a long time I was very unhappy.
Then one night I had a dream: I was to become a bride of

Jesus again. Shocked, I realized that I was no longer a bride. The Bible reading that same day confirmed it: "Nevertheless I have somewhat against thee, because thou hast left thy first love" (Rev. 2: 4). At last I submitted myself to the judgment of God and let His voice enter my heart; and what happened? Rev. 3: 20 gives the answer: "If anyone hears my voice and opens the door, I will come in to him and eat with him, and he with me."

At that time I had several quiet days and these were times when Jesus knocked at the door—far more than in the earlier days when I had known Him. Nothing else mattered—reading, walking, eating or sleeping. The hours sped away, for Jesus was there.

Sister of Mary Eusebia

I WANT YOU COMPLETELY

My Lord and my Bridegroom knocked tenderly and begged: "Give Me more of your time. I must have more of your time I must have more room in your heart. I want to take you more completely into My possession!" What did the Lord want? Did He want more than the normal times of prayer? This inner questioning held me fast. I felt Jesus' demand for love. I felt His pleas and longing. He wanted me to come more deeply into His fellowship. He wanted me to come apart and give myself only to Him.

How could I resist Him and His wooing? He is Love eternal. He is the fairest of the sons of men. In His royal majesty He inclines Himself to sinners and wants them in love to give themselves entirely to Him. So I went into the quietness for a few hours every day, and the Lord in His grace helped me to get my work done. Even then His urging did not cease; His love was still not satisfied. So I began to devote every Friday to Him, and when thus I tore myself away from my work and from many other things, He rewarded me with His loving presence which I had never known before.

I felt His love, which burns like a fire, which is stronger than any human love, because it comes straight from God's throne. It blazes out of His heart, which gave birth to all the fiery passion of the whole universe. I felt His love, intimate and tender, as no human love could possibly be. I felt His love, which is called "the river of thy delights" in Psalm 36: 8. This love was irresistible; it drew me closer and closer to Him. It called me to give myself to Him alone.

If I spent so much time apart with Him, would not this mean the neglect of my spiritual daughters, who had been entrusted to me? Would not Mother Martyria have to carry more of the burden? Would not much of the work which He had given me remain unfinished? He taught me that we must "abide in Him", love Him above all things with all our heart, with all our soul, with all our strength. We must follow the call of His love. We must go wherever He leads. The richest fruit can come only from such a union of love (John 15: 5). Only then will they be fully blessed who are entrusted to us.

So it happened, against all human expectation. My spiritual daughters wept at first, because I was less often among them. But after a few months they were no longer sad; they were happy. They had found that when I followed this way a new stream of life flowed forth to them. When we were together, Jesus was so truly there that He blessed us and appeared to us as never before. From that time they felt that Jesus was real and alive for them—whether He appeared as the Child in the manger, the Man of Sorrows or the risen Lord. His love waxed great among them. Their lives were renewed from the foundations and they were richer than they had ever been before. Jesus seemed to have made my daughters poorer by taking me away from them; but He did that in order to make them richer and happier.

And my work? Now it came to pass that the Lord permitted me to write everything, whether letters or books, in an entirely different way—in union with Him. So they reached the hearts of people more and more. Just as the Lord had told me; so it happened; from the quietness of the small room where I was alone with Him in prayer, the message travelled further still, and the effect was much greater than it would have been if I had just gone about my normal work. In this time of "seclusion" my writings spread throughout the land, and by means of my "seclusion" I reached thousands more in many lands, who gained a blessing through my work, than if I had just laboured with my Sisters on Canaan.

I see the wisdom of it all, Jesus is Love. If He calls someone to Himself, He will furnish him with all he needs. If He calls to us: "Give up the fellowship of those you love; give up the things you have been doing!" He will repay us a hundredfold. We have known this as we have lived together in the Sisterhood with Him the centre. More than all this; He will give us eternal divine life, His love, which is a brimming stream.

Mother Basilea

THE LORD IS A JEALOUS GOD (Exod. 34: 15)

Three short weeks in which to bring the gospel of Jesus to India! The timetable for my trip was very crowded.

Yet, with all the Sisters and hundreds of friends praying that I might be given strength, I had an accident, a fall, which greatly curtailed my activity. The doctor would not let me go any further. What a grief that was! Meetings which had been planned weeks ago would have to be cancelled.

I had been working without a stop, and sometimes gave five or six lectures in one day. Now here I was with two days of complete rest and quiet, and this at the one place in the whole of my Indian journeys that was suitable for such recuperation: it was in a large estate belonging to a brotherhood and sisterhood, just outside a remote South Indian village. On the first of these days I read this verse: "This is my beloved and this is my friend, O daughters of Jerusalem" (Song of Solomon, 5: 16b). Jesus, my Friend and Bridegroom, was waiting for my love. He wanted to have me to Himself during these days, my prayers, my love, my whole being. Jesus, the Bridegroom, loves us so much: He had such longing for fellowship with His bride that He called her from her work, so that He might have her all to Himself!

A little later we learned that it was fortunate that we had not met with the groups that were waiting for us. Our ministry there would not have been profitable. How unbelievably wonderful are our Lord's plans! He allowed these arrangements to be made as part of the India trip. Then He allowed them to lapse, so that I might go aside with Him—and at just the right place! In His holy revelation on Mount Sinai He said: "I the Lord your God am a jealous God!" (Exod. 20: 5).

Mother Basilea

I AM WAITING FOR YOU

Many of our visitors have told us that the best day of a retreat is the "Quiet Day". They are much impressed to begin with, when they open their door in the morning and find a small streamer bearing the words: *"I am waiting for you!"* Many of them thus realize for the first time: I am not primarily the one who has been longing for this encounter—no, it is Jesus who has been yearning for me.

This fact, that Jesus longs to have fellowship with us, was emphasized during the first years of the Sisterhood. When the first stage of our building scheme was finished, we lived together in very cramped quarters in our mother house. Some of us had to sleep in bunk beds. The number of occupants was based on the available space, not by the need for quiet. It certainly helped us to learn how to get along with each other! But there was a growing desire for a "prayer

closet". Our Mothers spoke with God about this. Je[..]
told us to enter our "closet" (AV) and close the door whe[..]
we wanted to pray (Matt. 6: 6). Now, God gave them the
assurance that Jesus would make this possible for us: there
would be an extension to the mother house, with only small
single rooms.

Everything about this second stage of our building pro-
gramme made a deep impression upon us. We have had several building projects, but this was the only one where the
money just rolled in to cover all the costs—without our
having to fight special battles of faith. We had never known
this before. It seemed as though this extension with its small
single rooms was especially pleasing to the Lord. It was like
a dream.

We shall never forget the day when we moved in. We
walked through the house singing songs of adoration. In
each room, beneath the crucifix Mother Basilea had placed a
streamer with the words: "I am waiting for you!" Yes, He
does really wait.

This why our guest house "Jesus' Joy" is nearly all single
rooms, and since then everyone is given this saying, "I am
waiting for you" at the beginning of a Quiet Day.

Sister of Mary Eulalia

THEY SAW NO MAN . . .
   SAVE JESUS ONLY (Mark 9: 8 AV)

During the preparation for Mother Basilea's trip to India a
great deal of literature about that country came into our
hands. It moved us deeply: what an unimaginable weight of
human suffering, expressed by word and picture! Then we
got the first long report from India. The Sister who accompanied Mother Basilea on this trip wrote about the same
misery—but from a different point of view. ". . . On an Indian holiday a cow was decorated and led through the
streets. Thousands of people were carried away by their

jubilation and enthusiasm. But the Christians seemed un-enthusiastic and joyless, and this grieved Mother Basilea deeply. A pitiful animal was given more honour and exal-tation than our Lord Jesus was accorded by His Christians. People starve that animals may live, while we offer such paltry sacrifices to Jesus . . ."

Again and again in the reports this point was made, and it moved us deeply. Surely it is the way things must appear to those who greatly love Jesus. We ought to try to see every-thing through the eyes and heart of the Beloved. Our view of things should no longer be horizontal, but vertical!

In the violence of the urge to destroy, in the protests of some young people against every form of authority, those who love Jesus can discern the hidden but very real rebellion against God. Others often see only actual happenings.

We sat in a circle, while a young student told us about the conditions in her dormitory. Everyone saw what a problem these things were. But the next evening, as we sat there again, the same girl told us just how Mother Basilea's lesson that morning had given her new vision. "Until this morning I had only seen the human aspect of these things, and the misery they cause. This morning I understood for the first time how these things make Jesus suffer."

Sister of Mary Rebekka

DO YOU LOVE ME?

Apart from the fact that I sought to love Jesus and had given up for Him everything of which my life had previously con-sisted—family, profession, freedom—I knew nothing, when I entered the Sisterhood of Mary.

Moreover, my first enthusiasm began to wane when I began to realize how much this way of life was costing me. Gradually I ceased to struggle to maintain my personal life of devotion and at the same time I ceased to strive in prayer for the task to which I had been called. One day everything seemed to be finished. But not for Jesus! "But do you not love Jesus?" That was the question which pierced my heart. Someone who did love Jesus asked me this, with great love.

"But do you not love Jesus?" In the light of this question I began a new life. In the light of this question everything which had previously been a burden suddenly became easy. Everything which had gone against the grain for me was suddenly worth while. Whenever anything threatened to overwhelm me, the same question presented itself: "But do you not love Jesus?", and in the light of the answer: "Yes, I love You," His saying was fulfilled: "My yoke is easy, and my burden is light" (Matt. 11: 30).

Sister of Mary Claudia

There was a special time of trial in my life, and it was several years later before I realized how fortunate I was that Jesus is such a jealous Lord in His love. For a time I had a task on Canaan which gave me much satisfaction. I was completely immersed in it. I loved it. I could arrange things and organize things. It was my whole joy. But suddenly, Jesus said "no" to this work. I was given a different job, because I had done my work well enough, but in a human way and not in a spiritual way. I was self-righteous about all this and I wallowed in my bitter thoughts. I felt that Jesus had not fulfilled my hopes, that He no longer loved me, that He had forgotten me.

The truth was exactly the opposite. His light of truth illumined my darkness until, full of contrition and shame I had to admit: I have forgotten You. I have not loved You above all else. I have not loved You more than my work, more than myself. Your love sought me in judgment and chastisement, because I had said "I want to love You above all else." Then I understood. I had to weep and mourn; I had to find my way back to Him, who loved me so jealously that He could not accept a divided love. Rejoicing, yet with tears,

I asked: "Why me? Why does He love me?" I cannot understand how You can love me, a sinner, and how it is that I may return Your love!

Sister of Mary Gabriele

MY BELOVED HAD TURNED AND GONE
   (Song of Solomon 5: 6)

We should praise the Lord whenever He gives us suffering because He has seen we are giving our love to men and to our work rather than to Him. How strong and full a love must be, if it would rather chastise us and cause us to suffer than to stand by and allow the slightest diminution of our love! How blessed are those who are loved so much that apparently harmless things might affect so close a relationship!

A holiday away in the quiet countryside! Days of Prayer! How long I had looked forward to this! They were intended as days of preparation for an important new chapter of my life. Alas! my happiness soon burned into deep disappointment. The quiet which I had yearned for proved to be empty, and my prayers seemed to rebound off the ceiling of the cold room. The Bible no longer spoke to me. I did not understand what God was doing. Was I not here just to listen to Him?

A verse from Micah 7 was my answer: "I will bear the indignation of the Lord, because I have sinned against Him" (v. 9). I recalled the past weeks. I had been very busy. The work had so engrossed me that I was already thinking about it during the morning Bible study. I had hardly thought of God all day. Any spare time I got I spent with a dear friend who was visiting me.

"Abide in Me!" Was that not the the commandment which Jesus had given us in His great love? How I must have hurt Him! Unrequited love is one of the most painful things in life! I had treated Jesus like that. Deeply shocked, I could realize how wonderful it is that He wants to have us with Him always, because He loves us so. I realized too that His desire for our love is holy—if I do not desire to be with Him, He cannot be with me. So I was able humbly to accept these days in the spiritual "desert".

Sister of Mary Dolores

IT WAS GRANTED HER TO BE CLOTHED WITH FINE LINEN, BRIGHT AND PURE (Rev. 19: 8)

It must be thirty years ago now that I was looking through some fashion magazines. I turned page after page, looking for the wedding dress which I thought I would like to wear some day. At last I found one that satisfied me. It was a long robe, simple in style. Marvellous! Wonderful! I wanted to greet my bridegroom on our wedding day wearing this dress, to give him happiness. I dreamed of great, strong love, a mutual giving and receiving, of being one in outlook, of being completely filled with "you". I met many fine people who made life interesting for me and gave me worthwhile activities. But I did not find what I was looking for. In my longing for satisfaction I gave myself very fully to a number of friends and occupied myself with them. But really I was lonely. Years later, while I was tidying up one day, I found that page from the fashion magazine. "My" wedding dress had turned yellow! I threw the paper away. It did not seem likely that the love I was still seeking did really exist—or did it?

A few years ago I took part in a pilgrimage to Ranft, in Switzerland, in the valley where Nicholas von der Flüe had lived. He had become a hermit in order to live sacrificially out of love for his Lord. Though many years had passed the whole atmosphere of his hermitage breathed this spirit of dedication and prayer. There in the quiet the crucifix on the wall began to speak to me of a love which was still waiting for me, of this Jesus who had been my Companion from my youth and had remained faithful to me even when I went astray.

I cannot remember how I came out of the valley of Ranft. But I knew that I could no longer evade this demand for love. I must leave the things I loved most so that I might realize this great love which had waited so long for me in vain. I must follow Him, no matter where He led me. He led me into the Sisterhood of Mary.

Jesus did not appear to me at the very beginning as the Bridegroom. I could not approach Him as I was then—so sure of myself and so "pious". The old rage which had served to cover my nakedness and my sore spots had to be torn away. When I realized how ugly I was, when I could find nothing beautiful in myself, when I could only cry for mercy in my misery of sin, He came to me, He whom I love so intimately today. I saw how sorely He suffered for my sake—and then He drew me to Himself.

If anyone asks me nowadays: "Is there really such a thing as this great love, which can satisfy you completely? Does this love of which you had dreamed really exist?" My soul rejoices as I answer: "Yes, there is such a love! A thousand times more beautiful than I had longed for. This love cannot be compared with human love. It is so tender and pure, so refreshing, so comforting, so full of understanding. This love never disappoints. It is stronger than death. It draws me into heaven. Yes, this love is leading me to the wedding!"

Wedding? I remember once more my wedding dress that had turned yellow. I no longer need it. For this wedding, for the marriage of the Lamb, I do not have to prepare my own wedding dress. I believe that an even more beautiful one will have been prepared for me—one that is woven out of much suffering and washed in the blood of the Lamb. This dress will never turn yellow, not through all eternity! Its purity will forever reveal the infinite love of Jesus.

Sister of Mary Nicola

O Jesus, Lamb of God, most fair,
My Bridegroom, Lord and Friend most dear,
A heart of love I offer.

Who is like You, my dearest Lord?
For ever may You be adored
By me beyond all other!

Your richest gifts You ever pour
Out of Your heavenly treasure store
On me, the chief of sinners.

I worship You with loving heart
For You in boundless love impart
Such overwhelming blessing.

True treasure, joy Your love will supply;
The heavenly kingdom is brought nigh.
My thankful heart I give You.

WJ 222